The Women's Little Black Book for Strutting Out of Stress

How To Kick The "S"Out of Stress!

Samantha Tubbs-Crews, LMHC

Book Cover by Vicente Mendoza (Fiverr)

Library of Congress Control Number: 2024913033
How to Kick The "S" Out of Stress! The Women's Little Black Book for Strutting Out
of Stress/Samantha Tubbs-Crews

ISBN 979-8-9905933-0-5 (Paperback)
ISBN 979-8-9905933-1-2 (eBook)

Printed in the United States of America

TABLE OF CONTENTS

This book is dedicated to my mother who is now resting in heaven. I started writing this book in 2020 only a few months before she earned her heavenly wings.

Although I took some necessary pauses, Mom, the persistence and confidence you instilled in me helped me to make it to the finish line with this book. Thank you for all the love you have given me and every lesson you have taught me. You will forever be the Queen of my heart!

ACKNOWLEDGEMENTS

I would first like to thank my Creator and Heavenly Father who gifted me with the knowledge to write this book and to be a chosen vessel in which to encourage others. I am so grateful to have so many people in my life who support me and inspire me. To all of my family, I am so grateful for your loving presence in my life. It would take up a whole chapter in this book for me to list the names of all the people who have made such a wonderful impact in my life.

To my husband, Patrick and our oldest son, Julius, I extend the utmost love and thanks to the both of you for unwavering belief and encouragement from the first moment I began the process of writing. You are the best two cheerleaders that anyone can have!

I want to especially thank my invaluable editing team; Casey Curry, Author and Retired Educator and Carol Caruso, Retired Licensed Mental Health Counselor for providing me with your assistance and scholarly insights. My respect and admiration for authors has definitely risen as I have come to learn that writing and self publishing a book is not as easy as it may seem.

To my new beautiful daughter-in-love, Monique Tubbs, I sincerely appreciate your resourcefulness and expertise in the area of exercise and fitness.

I also want to express much gratitude to Dr. Lorraine Reeves, Author and Educator; and to Marion Huey, Licensed Mental Health Counselor for the awesome book reviews!

Lastly, but never least, "thank you" seems like such a small word to express my gratitude to one of my forever besties, Vanessa Russell, for such a touching Foreword. I must admit, I was not prepared when I read it. I smiled, I cried, I laughed and I love it! It certainly sums up the depth of our friendship over the many years. I am very much looking forward to writing your Foreword soon!

FOREWORD

From childhood antics and school shenanigans; to college; lucrative careers; dysfunctional relationships, life as an overly confident single professional, to happily married with kids living our best middle class life, to struggling through bouts of depression; recessions; seasons of abundant faith, to sometimes no faith at all; Samantha Tubbs-Crews, has been "my person" through it all. In fact, even while typing this, I'm trying to recall my life memories without her in them!

Over 40 years of 'tried and proven' friendship, Sam, as I affectionately call her, has literally been there with me in every facet of my life, from our childhood to now! Her calm, always poised position of strength and non-judgmental approach to meet you right where you are, is just one of the things I love most about her and makes her such a phenomenal psychotherapist!

Her intuitive ability to really listen, and help you find your breath is profound, as she guides you to peace in her tranquil tone; "Nell, a personal nickname only my family calls me, "tell me what you are feeling; now tell me what makes you feel this way," she will ask, then something to the effect, "are you ready to release that?" I've always admired her strategic skills as a licensed mental health counselor/psychotherapist where she doesn't tell you what to do or think, rather she allows you to see what you have always been doing, then assists you in changing the narrative! This is exactly what she does in this inspired, new book!

Sam engages the reader to discover their own truth and what triggers their stress! I'm excitedly pausing at the moment, as I realize how many years of free therapy I've received because of our longevity, and how so many people will be empowered by her priceless wisdom and expertise now on the pages of her very own book! And what a book it is! The title alone captures the essence of what Sam has been showing clients, audiences, professional colleagues and friends to do all along!!!

Stress has taken the lead in our lives for far too long! And If you're ready to embark on a journey of gentleness with yourself, and the ones you love; if you're ready to walk in the peace and inner joy you deserve, please keep reading because my girlfriend, sis, bestie; my person; a compassionate expert with over 29 years in mental health counseling; has been called to guide us all!!

Vanessa Kaye Russell, Emmy Award-Winning Producer
(a.k.a. "Jumpsuit" a Sam/Vanessa joke)

INTRODUCTION

L et's face it, stress is a part of life!!! A woman's to-do list seems to be never ending, right? So much to do and so little time. As "high-definition" women we tend to take stress to the next level. I termed the concept of a high-definition woman as one who is always extending upward to a greater distance than what is usually expected from many men. We take on way too much, we are harder on ourselves, we often compare ourselves to other women and we don't use the word "No" enough. In some cases, we overextend ourselves to try to please everyone else but only to realize that no one ended up happy.

It's amazing how stress can just show up out of nowhere sometimes. It is experienced often when there is a lot on our plate, and we feel pressured to handle everything on that plate all at once. Stress is no stranger to women, especially for women who are high-definition aka high achievers and take pride in being able to juggle so many responsibilities and obligations at the same time.

What a grand entrance stress tends to make in many of our lives as mothers, wives, career builders, entrepreneurs, and caregivers. The list really could go on and on. For most women, the more responsibilities taken on, the more stress that is encountered. Stress comes in all shapes and sizes. It can affect you physically and mentally. It has no specific time frame to come or leave. It also affects every woman differently. As challenging as stress can be to deal with at times, it can also become habitual unknowingly.

I imagine if I had the honor to introduce "Stress" at a women's banquet it would be in this fashion, "Women, this next guest needs no introduction and is very familiar to us all. This guest has starred in numerous events, but often making the most appearances in workplaces, homes, and social settings. This guest is noted for producing feelings of frustration, lack of confidence, feelings of insecurity, depression, anxiety, and overwhelm. Women are frequented by this guest more than men and lastly this guest's motto is "The more you are with me, the more you are willing to keep me around. Ladies, I present to you this Woman of Distinction – "Ms. Stress to Impress." If it sounds like you have been hanging out with this guest, it could very well be a love hate relationship. Let me tell you, the internal struggle is real! In the upcoming chapters, you will learn more about constructive ways to manage life stressors and practical strategies to help you strut right out of your stress!

CHAPTER ONE

WHAT IS LEFT WHEN THE "S" IS GONE - TRESS!

S tress is a normal reaction from the brain and body when you are faced with attempting to accomplish a demand or challenge. As mentioned in the introduction, stress can also be experienced when you have too much on your plate and you are pressured to get everything on your plate completed all at once. Managing stress in a healthy way is key when life events place so many demands on us. Just imagine what possibilities are waiting for you once you release the "S" from your life.

So, what is this "TRESS" you would be delighted to have and how will it make such a big difference in your life? Well first off, the word Tress is defined as a braid, knot, curl or hair. It is described in synonym form as a secure hold; a form of control. When I connected these two concepts together it really made me think about how stress can be such a strong force in many women's lives today. Stress can absolutely cause your stomach to turn into knots and can even sometimes have you curled over in a dark corner in your room in just the same way your hair curls.

Of course, you can't avoid stress all together, but you can take some steps in your life to lessen the impact that stress has on your life. You can also be more intentional about engaging in activities that honor you and your well-being. After kicking the "s" out of stress, your strength can now be drawn from a repurposed acronym for TRESS!

T – Time to focus on yourself

R – Relax

E – Exercise

S – Set realistic expectations of yourself

S – Set personal boundaries

I will go into detail in the remaining chapters to explain how to utilize each component of TRESS as a strategy to help you say goodbye to the strong hold that stress has on you and to help you take control of your life!

This book is written specifically for women because we tend to have more stressors in our lives. It's not that men don't get stressed; however, women experience higher levels of stress because of the traditional support roles we play as wives and mothers, and the stresses of hands-on parenting, as well as the way we are socialized to say yes as an extension of being "nice."

It's also important to mention that men and women handle stress differently. Women are more likely to internalize stress, leading more readily to both physical and mental disorders, while men tend to externalize it in the form of aggression or impulsivity. When you consider the long list of responsibilities women tend to have and the various roles played, it is understandable that our stress levels are higher. Researchers are also discovering that hormones, as well as other aspects of physiology can have a major impact on how women's bodies respond to stress.

Over my 29 years of working in the mental health field, I have collected many useful tools and created some of my own for managing stress, so I hope you will find this book helpful on your journey to kicking the "s" out of the stress in your life.

My Lemonade Story

Every woman can recall an experience where stress took over and you felt totally out of control! What does it even feel like to be stressed or out of control? Well, I can tell you how it felt for me during a time in my life where I felt EVERYTHING was falling to pieces. I was in my late 20's and in the middle of a divorce. This was my first real dance with despair. I was facing legal challenges, financial hardship, and parenting crises all at the same time. Where it seemed like my life should have just gotten started, in reality, my life was in a quick decline.

Even though I had completed my mental health counseling degree and was preparing for licensure, I began to feel discouraged. I couldn't sleep, didn't have much of an appetite, felt depressed, embarrassed, uncertain, and inadequate. Prior to the curve ball that I was thrown, I was so excited about the possibility of being able to establish a private practice. I had been working in the mental health field since my mid-twenties but found myself at a place of questioning if I could even offer anyone anything of value when I was in such a state of turmoil. Would anyone take me seriously? Would I still be acknowledged as credible? Could I continue moving forward in my career despite not being able to exemplify the very thing that I was expected to help others with?

I remember talking to one of my best friends about my dilemma. I told her that I was thinking about possibly switching gears in my career. After all, it was already off to a bad start! I had been in the role of providing encouragement, motivation, inspiration, and coping skills, but did any of those skills help my current situation? My confidence level was at an all-time low.

After sharing with my friend that people would look at where I am and not feel that I could be of any help to them in the least bit, my friend said to me, "How do you know if what you are facing right now won't be such a blessing to other women who may be going through the same thing now or in the future?" I had a connection moment that day! I would definitely know what it feels like to go through a divorce and could provide support in that area. I could certainly relate! So, this is how I started mixing my lemonade: I did pause from seeing couples for a while to do some self-care, but I continued my work with individual clients and began to include a divorce recovery focused clientele.

If I would have changed my career or continued to feel like I didn't have anything to offer anyone anymore, I would have missed an opportunity to help many women going through a divorce. I would have also missed the opportunity to help couples work through the kinks in their marriages. I also had to remind myself that this would not be the last time that I would be facing something stressful in my life! The lesson I learned then as a therapist was, I didn't have to be perfect in order to help others. I needed to allow myself to feel my pain, deal with my pain, so I could heal from my pain.

Stressful times can certainly throw some sour lemons your way but it's not the lemons that determine the quality of your life; in fact, it's what you do with the lemons that truly define your destiny. The lemons serve a purpose that we don't tend to see or like at the time we are enduring the stress in our lives.

Getting back to the example of my lemonade situation, stress motivated me to admit that I was human and in emotional pain; but that I can still be professional, purposeful, and impactful! I gave myself the time and grace that I needed to recover. I utilized the support of family, friends, colleagues, church, and professional counseling to help me stir up what would become a refreshing batch of lemonade.

Oftentimes women ignore the signs of stress. There is way too much to do and very little time to complete the undated requests demanded of our time. It can also be easy to dismiss signs of stress if you are not familiar with them. Stress comes in various forms and it affects every woman differently. Signs of stress can present themselves physically and mentally as they did in my case. The next page will highlight some warning signs of stress.

HOW TO RECOGNIZE COMMON SIGNS OF STRESS

Mental Alarms	Physical Alarms
Easily annoyed	Headaches
Difficulty concentrating	Constipation
Mind going blank	Diarrhea
Suicidal thoughts	Difficulty sleeping
Feeling insecure	Excessive sweating
Indecisiveness	Nausea
Worrying	Lack of energy
Depression	Muscle tightness
Lack of motivation	Dizziness
Low sexual desire	Grinding teeth
Negative thinking	Heartburn
Crying	Shakiness
Lack of enjoyment	Sexual problems
Isolation	Loss of appetite
Avoidance	Overeating
	Aggravation of existing medical conditions
	skin problems

As you can see from the list of common signs of stress, it can definitely have an influence on your daily functioning. Knowing how stress affects you is only half of the battle. Learning what to do about the stress is where the victory lap comes in!

I don't want you to think all stress is bad though! Some stress can actually be beneficial. As a matter of fact, stress can be both motivating and protective. If there is a particular task or goal that you want to complete, stress can serve as a motivator. It can propel you to focus and be more aware of the time that you have to complete the task or goal.

Stress can equally help you push through some situations and events, even when you don't feel like it. That's where resilience comes in! With the many responsibilities that you face, without that extra twinge of motivation, certain tasks, or goals that you want to accomplish would simply be pushed to the side – gone and forgotten!

When it comes to job promotions, career opportunities, sporting events, or getting your groove back, positive/healthy stress plays a role in gaining a competitive edge. By the same token, stress serves as a protector against situations that could be potentially dangerous. For instance, if a car was driving in your direction and it looked like you were going to be hit, stress signals (sounds, images), would create a response in your body that will allow you to quickly react to avoid being run over by the car. In this case, cortisol, which is the primary stress hormone, is suddenly elevated and helps to regulate your body's stress response. After the danger of being hit by a car has passed, the cortisol level typically decreases.

It's important to point out though, when stress is long-term (chronic) or excessive; that's when it is not considered as beneficial but rather harmful. If cortisol levels remain high in the body for prolonged periods of time, it can put your health at risk.

In today's busy world where the demands upon women are so high and women are met with the overwhelming responsibilities of balancing careers, family life, personal life, and social life, it can be hard to even notice when the pressures of life are taking a toll on you. It can be easy to just jump in auto pilot and keep things moving along.

You may not realize the changes that affect your body or your mind over time. Of course, every woman experiences stress differently so self-awareness is key for overcoming stress. What may cause one woman to lose sleep may not affect another woman at all.

The top 7 causes of stress:
Death of a loved one
Divorce and relationship challenges
Loss of a job
Increased financial obligations
Getting married
Moving into a new home
Chronic Illness

The Ultimate Stressor of 2020

I can't truly say enough about that unforgettable year and how it re-shaped our whole world. The end of 2019, the world was faced with a pandemic known as COVID-19. When we reflect back on that time, it reminds us of how stressful it was and to some degree, the stress still continues! As I write this book, four years later, we are still dealing with COVID-19, but certainly not to the level that it started out.

In the beginning of the pandemic, we did not really know a lot about it or how to protect ourselves from it. It was a long and scary road for most people. As time went on, we learned about safety measures we could take to protect ourselves and others. Think about the huge adjustment that had to be made in most people's lives. Working from home with family and pets around daily, technology reliance, home schooling, isolation from family, friends, and co-workers. Unfortunately, handshakes and hugs were strongly advised against as protective measures. Trying to figure out how to get groceries and toiletries safely became a major stressor.

Our social events, exercise centers, and spiritual activities were at a halt until we learned how to connect virtually. Hair and nail grooming routines were frantically disrupted. There were even many daycare centers that were not in operation. Sadly, according to the Center for Disease Control and Prevention (CDC), millions of lives were claimed by the virus in the United States alone.

On a daily basis, I remember speaking to so many people who were devastated by all of the challenges we faced in the beginning of the pandemic. For so many of us, we had never experienced anything like this in our lives. Our bearings were knocked from under us. Even though we are hedging toward the recovery stages now and the world has opened back up, it is still very difficult and scary for many people.

The projected adjustments continue as we have now returned back to work in office buildings; our school-aged kids have resumed attending brick and mortar schools, our pets are missing us throughout the day, the anxiety of taking our small kids back to daycare again is high, and the frustration of driving in heavy traffic has returned. Stress management is monumental in dealing with such a huge disruption of life. Unraveling all the layers of stress can be complex but owning and labeling your experiences with stress is a big start to managing the stress.

Now that you know stress can make its grand entrance into your life at any time, it's time to understand what your stressors are. Women, we have to pay attention to the things that get us emotionally charged so that we can keep our stress in check. As high-definition women, it is important to recognize that while anything is possible – not everything is possible!

Think about some of the situations that are going on in your life right now. Is it job dissatisfaction? Increase in job responsibilities? Relationship or Marital Problems? Parenting Responsibilities? Financial Debt? Medical problems? Caregiving of an Elderly Parent? Loss of a loved one? or Pandemic Aftermath? Chances are, there is at least one of these situations occurring in your life this very moment. Chances are you are experiencing several of the listed symptoms of stress at this very moment.

Whether you checked off one symptom or all of them, the effects of stress can interfere with your daily life if it goes unnoticed and unmanaged. Keep this gem in mind, it's not the stress that creates the biggest problem in our lives, it's our response to the stressors that really trips us up! When you are facing some real challenging times, think about how you deal with the stress. There are constructive and destructive ways of coping with stress.

For example, if you have a bad day at work, what's the first thing that you think of doing when you get home? Depending on how you answered, your way of coping may have made your situation worse. Coping constructively entails engaging in positive activities and/or a positive mindset that allows you to get through a situation in a helpful manner. For example, exercising, calling a friend, or listening to music would be considered as coping constructively. On the other hand, coping destructively is engaging in self-defeating activities and/or a self-defeating mindset that prevents you from managing your situation effectively. In this case, it means the way in which you deal with your situation is harmful to yourself or others. Subsequently, using alcohol to escape reality, yelling at the kids, or excessive shopping are destructive ways to cope with stress.

Once you are aware of your stressors and how they impact your life, YOU can decide to change how you respond to lessen the effects of stress. You are happier, and more fulfilled and not weighted down with disappointment when you know ahead of time what YOU can actually do to manage your stress and what you need to avoid doing! On the next page you will find a

Stress Response Inventory that can assist you in identifying your stressor and developing a plan of action that you can be proud of.

My Stress Response Inventory

Physical Symptom (s):

Mental Symptoms (s):

How I cope(d):

Was my coping style constructive (helpful) or destructive (harmful)?

Is/Was the situation inside or outside of my control?

Identify any part of the situation that is/was within my control?

Lemonade Moment: What can I do to improve my situation now or in the future?

Emotion Calibration and Regulation

As you are learning, managing stress has a lot to do with how you view or assess your stressor. Is your situation more like a carpet spill or a house fire? Let's be honest, sometimes mountains can be made from molehills. You may take something relatively small and hype it up in your mind to make it seem larger than life itself. One way you can avoid this mishap is to apply this handy little strategy. On a scale of 0 – 10, rate how big of an impact your SITUATION is with 0 being none and 10 being the highest level. Notice, I did not ask you to rate how big or heavy your emotions feel. There is an important reason you are not asked to rate your emotions.

Your emotions may sometimes inadequately reflect the situation at hand. Emotions are automatic and they trigger or motivate behavior. If you rate how big or heavy your emotion feels as a guide to handle problems, then you may be misguided and prone to over-react quite a bit. However, if you really think about your situation and rate it on a scale of 0 – 10 as to how big of an impact the situation is on your life, you are more likely to manage your situation in a more constructive manner. The closer your rating is to a 0, the more likely your situation is to be closer to a carpet spill, which isn't really a big deal. Chances are, you are able to regulate your emotion to match the situation. The closer your rating is to a 10, then your situation is one that is of urgency, similar to a house fire. Very few situations will be on the higher end of the scale on a day-to-day basis, which means that for most of the time, your situation can be managed without the extra intensity added. Here is a guide to help you execute an action plan that is appropriate for dealing with your situation.

0 - 3 = Not that big of a deal. Regulation Tool: Make a decision to move on and don't give the situation much energy. In other words, don't sweat the small stuff. Shift your focus to something else that really deserves your

attention more, even if that something else is you. Sometimes you have to just have to B.R.E.A.T.H.E through the moment. I thought I might stop here to make sure you know what it means to breathe or take a cleansing breath and how to do so. You start by breathing in through your nose and fill your belly all the way up with air as if it was inflating like a balloon. Then when you cannot breathe in any more air, you simply release it as if you are emptying your lungs. To help you remember the power of breathing through the moment, I came up with this neat little mantra, "Be Really Enlightened About Thoughts Having Exit-space." This concept enforces the mindset that whenever you have distressing or self-defeating thoughts, you can remind yourself that they don't have to stay. I'm sure there are activities, projects, errands or just listening to relaxing music that will benefit you way more than stewing over something that stands in the way of your peace. What is the likelihood that holding on to this issue is going to make you feel better? Giving yourself or someone else grace and forgiveness may be a good way to prevent yourself from being emotionally incarcerated.

4 - 7 = Important but not the end of the world that the situation happened or did not happen. Regulation Tool: Explore what steps may be needed to address the issue. This is where healthy coping tools also come into play such as journaling down your thoughts and feelings rather than reacting, having a conversation to talk over the situation with someone, or establish boundaries that protect against the situation from occurring again.

8 - 10 = Urgent matter. Regulation Tool: Take a deep breath and stay calm! Assess if you or anyone else is in any danger. Assess if you are sick or hurt. Does the urgent matter require you to respond on someone else's behalf such as rendering CPR? The theme of safety and quick level headed action should be the focus in this category. Your urgent matter may require medical attention, crucial home repairs, financial or legal assistance, etc. Your response can vary from handling matters on your own to contacting

911 or local law enforcement. It may also be a good idea to have someone accompany you or drive for you in cases where transportation is needed if you are too overwhelmed to drive for yourself. And of course, if you are religious, you can never go wrong with saying a quick prayer. I want to make sure there is a clear understanding of what types of events typically are seen as urgent. This understanding can be extremely helpful when trying to apply the rating scale to your situation. Of course, if your house is truly on fire, then by all means, safety and exiting your home should be your first priority! True emergency matters can range from varying degrees so your response will also vary.

CHAPTER TWO

YOUR CUP COULD USE A REFILL

TAKE TIME TO FOCUS ON YOURSELF

Now ladies even though you may be ready for that second round of coffee to get you through the day, I am not referring to any beverages at all! I am simply speaking of refilling your cup with YOU, imagine that! You may be asking, "what does it mean to fill your cup with you, and isn't that selfish?" I am sure you have seen cups with this sentiment written on it, "you can't pour from an empty cup!" This statement suggests that something must already be in the cup before you can pour anything from it. It also means that you would have to choose YOU first by placing you in the cup!

To further drive this point home, if you have ever traveled on a plane, prior to take off, you were given some wise instructions. You were told that in the likelihood of an emergency and the loss of aircraft pressure to immediately place the designated device over your face FIRST if you have children. Even the airlines get it, you can't help someone else if you are out of oxygen!!! Choosing you means making yourself a priority and being intentional in doing so.

Think about priorities that you may have in your life now that tend to involve other people. I suppose they are priorities because they are important to you; however, aren't you important to yourself? Priorities are concerns, interests and desires that come before anything else. When you make yourself a priority you are declaring your own self-worth! You are saying "I matter, and I am important! Placing value on your life does not make you conceited or selfish. Quite frankly, the way you treat yourself often serves as a model for how others treat you.

Depending on how you grew up and what you were taught, you may feel guilty about focusing on yourself. Societal norms and religion can sometimes make you feel that you have to put yourself on the back burner. Remember, making yourself a priority does not mean that you are only investing in yourself, it means that you are investing in yourself first before others!

Think about the last time you really allowed yourself to focus on your needs, goals, and dreams. Perhaps you have obligated yourself so much to others that you have not even made the time to reflect on what makes you happy. It is important to identify things in life that make you smile, laugh, or feel good about yourself. I would encourage you to take a self-care break now and list five things you enjoy doing.

Self-Care Time

Five things I enjoy doing: (Think of them as Petals of Joy)

1.

2.

3.

4.

5.

Record the approximate date of the last time you engaged in the activity and how it made you feel (next to it).

If after reviewing your list, you find that a lot of time has gone by since you have done any of those items, that could be a sign that you have gotten out of touch with yourself. Make a plan to incorporate those petals of joy into your life on a regular basis.

In order to fill your cup, knowing what to put in it is paramount. Identifying the things you enjoy doing is just the beginning of this process. Recognizing things you enjoy doing and highlighting some of your favorite things in life gives you somewhat of a road map on ways to honor yourself. Filling your cup and keeping it filled prevents you from experiencing burnout from work or home life. If your cup is going to overflow, let it run over with all the things that nourish the innermost part of your being.

I want you to think *only* about yourself for just a moment. Yes, I am giving you total permission to be selfish! I want you to think about what matters most to you on a small or large scale. When you think about exposing yourself to your most favorite things in life as often as you can, how does that feel to you? For me it's like giving myself a gift that I know I will love or simply pampering myself with all the things I know I will enjoy having. It gives me something to look forward to and something originated by me, for me, that nurtures me, and keeps me in touch with myself.

When you are intentional about doing things to make yourself happy, you are less dependent upon others to make you happy. If you are in the driver's seat, where you drive is up to you!

Crews Nugget #1: It is your responsibility to make yourself happy! This is where you hit "rewind and repeat again!" If you are finding that you are often frustrated by other people disappointing you or you are not getting the things you want out of life, then you may have delegated one of the most game changing tasks to someone who cannot fulfill it. Ladies, use your power for your own good. If you choose to turn over your keys to someone else and leave the driving to them, complaining about the destination, or even the route, is not fair to the person who is driving.

As a therapist with almost three decades of experience, I still cannot say that I've seen it all or heard it all! During this time, there were some common themes that I often observed as I counseled women. One of them being so many women who were very angry at someone else for the displeasure in their own life. Some of the common comments I heard were:

" If he/she would just....then I would be happy."

"He/she should know what it takes to make me happy by now!"

"I don't have time to do the things I want to because he/she needs me."

"I will finally be able to focus on my happiness once he/she is happy."

"He/she does not believe that I deserve to be happy."

One of my clients shared with me that she would finally be happy once the people in her life stopped having so many expectations of her. I asked her what did other people's expectations have to do with her happiness? I noticed the look that she had on her face. It was as if she had suddenly just been freed from a dark, lonely, empty room that she had been trapped inside of for years. As tears fell down her cheek, she said to me, "I have never looked at it that way. It always seemed to me that if people expected something of me, that I needed to make it happen. I never once considered that I actually had a choice." We can't stop other people from wanting or expecting us to do something. It is up to us to choose to do things that make us happy.

I have included an exercise for you to get to know yourself a little better. Taking the time to focus on what makes you tick, can be helpful to others in getting to know you better as well. This tool can also be utilized by others for special holidays, recognition events and "just because" acknowledgements when they may not be sure what to get for you. I also give this as a homework assignment to family members and couples to set aside some time for this exercise to learn more about each other. By keeping your original sheet and providing the other person(s) with a copy, you can make special moments so much more personal and even fun.

Of Course, It's All About *ME*!!!

My favorite color is:

My favorite restaurant is:

My favorite food is:

My favorite song is:

My favorite movie is:

My favorite candy bar is:

My favorite book is:

My favorite quote is:

My favorite entertainer is:

My favorite hobby is:

My favorite fragrance is:

My favorite sport is:

My favorite vacation is:

My favorite holiday is:

My favorite ways to feel loved are:

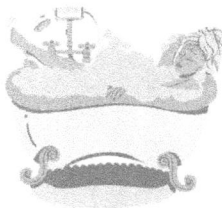

Intentional Positive Self-Talk

When you think about who you are, how do you describe yourself? What you say about yourself has a lot to do with how you handle your day-to-day activities. Your self-talk can play a major role in the stress that you may be encountering in your life. Your mind is the steering wheel for every direction in which you travel. You set the bar for what your aim is going to be relative to your goals in life, relationships, career, and finances, etc. One of my favorite quotes is "Whether you think you can, or think you can't, you're right", by Henry Ford.

Positive self-talk has to be an intentional thing because self-talk can work both ways. Positive self-talk can be a challenge for some people. "Self-talk," is an internal monologue or a person's inner voice. It can also be a narrative or commentary that you entertain about yourself, or it can be spoken aloud. Such narratives that are influenced by thoughts and beliefs that you hold about yourself can be very powerful. Different thoughts and beliefs that you hold about yourself can come from various sources.

Experiences from growing up, relationships, careers, religious affiliations, and other social affiliations are common avenues which can generate self-talk. If your self-talk is positive, then it is more likely that your level of self-confidence will be higher, your level of stress will be lower, your relationships will be more fulfilling and your life in general will be more satisfying. On the other hand, if your self-talk is negative, then you will be less likely to go after the things you really want out of life, which results in your life being less satisfying overall.

Depending on what you say to yourself about yourself, about your experiences or circumstances, it can make the difference on the outcome of your situation. Being intentional with the use of positive self-talk or compassionate self-talk helps you to train your thoughts to be positive to achieve better outcomes in life. Positive self-talk is also a great way to promote a positive self-image and improve your mood. If your mindset is a positive one, then you tend to feel better about yourself and the world, even if your experiences are not always the best.

I am not saying you have to downplay things or sugar coat your experiences, but perspective is everything! If there is a task that I need to perform and it is very challenging to me, I can tell myself "you are not smart enough to figure this out" or I can tell myself "I will do the best I can and use the resources I have to get this done." One train of thought will prevent me from even trying and the other train of thought will motivate me to at least do my best to accomplish the goal. What you tell yourself really does matter!

I want to encourage you to begin to take notice of any negative self-talk that you may be entertaining. The following page list a few examples of positive and negative self-talk to assist you in gaining a better understanding of how powerful your words really are.

Negative Self-Talk	Positive Self-Talk
• I will never measure up.	• I am good enough.
• I am such a dummy.	• I am smart.
• I am lazy.	• I am a hard worker.
• Love is just not meant for me.	• I am capable of giving and receiving love.
• I am a failure	• I will always do my best.
• I can't do this.	• I will get through this one day at a time.
• Things will always be horrible for me.	• Things will get better.
• I am not attractive.	• I am beautiful inside and out.
• No one cares about me.	• I have people in my life who love me and care about me.
• It's useless to go after this job, I won't get it anyway.	• I will prepare for the interview and do my best.

DO YOU HEAR THE WORDS THAT ARE COMING OUT OF YOUR MOUTH???

Would you say the type of negative things about your friends that you say to yourself? I would guess that most of you would never use the same critical evaluation of your friends that you tend to use toward yourself. Well, today all of the beating up on yourself and putting yourself down ends here!

Now that you have an idea of what not to say to yourself and about yourself, you have an opportunity in the space below to replace any negative statements about yourself with positive and/or compassionate self-talk. This is the kind of self-talk you can use to comfort, support, and motivate yourself just as you would for a good friend.

MY FRIENDSHIP SELF-TALK

I am:

I can:

I will:

The Big Takeaway

Generally speaking, we are all a product of the environments we grow up in whether those environments were positive or not so positive. It is possible and likely that the environment in which we grew up caused us to adopt "takeaways" that are still operating in our lives today. Sometimes we are aware of the takeaways as we get older but sometimes, we are not.

Takeaways are life lessons that we learn during our growing up years as well as during adulthood. If we experience something unpleasant or traumatic, we may walk away from that experience with a certain understanding about it that impacts our decision making, relationships with others, career choices, etc. The takeaways may be based on erroneous messages about ourselves, others or the world. For example, if you grew up in an abusive environment, your takeaway knowingly or unknowingly (subconsciously) could be, "it's not ok for me to speak up or I will be hurt" or it could be "being hit is the way my partner expresses their love for me."

One of the interesting things about takeaways is that you may not even be aware that you have adopted a takeaway but can still be using it to get your needs met or to protect yourself. Your takeaway could be one of a protective nature by declaring something to help you to avoid being hurt or to survive. In this case, your takeaway could be "I will never have children so that they won't suffer from abuse," or it could be, "I will never get married because I would be setting myself up for abuse." It would amaze you to know that your takeaway could even be "I can't trust anyone because people will hurt me," Furthermore, it could also be "the best way to get what I want is to hurt others."

The list could go on and on with various takeaways that may be erroneous. I feel it's important to say that not all takeaways are negative or erroneous. There are more positive takeaways that lead to living successful and fulfilling lives such as: "I will establish a savings account to put money away for a rainy day," "taking vacations will be a priority for me," or "I will be a loving and compassionate mother." It could also be "I will stand up for myself and not go along with things I am not happy with."

It can certainly be very stressful and disappointing when we are not living our best lives; therefore, careful examination of what might be standing in the way is vital. Using the Error Message Alert Exercise on the next page, write down any takeaways you may have adopted that may be holding you back from accomplishing your dreams, goals, career endeavors, or relationship pursuits. Once you have identified your takeaways, in the space under it, re-write your takeaway so that it motivates or empowers you.

If you find that you have more erroneous takeaways still operating than you realized, simply copy this format, and keep going. After all, if your takeaways are going to be leading some of your biggest life decisions, they should be positive, rational, and supportive.

Error Message Alert Exercise

1) Erroneous Takeaway:

1a) Empowerment Takeaway:

2) Erroneous Takeaway:

2a) Empowerment Takeaway:

3) Erroneous Takeaway:

3a) Empowerment Takeaway:

Intentionally Honoring Your Goals and Dreams

Seriously, how closely are you aligned with your goals and dreams? Because life can be so busy, goals can often be pushed off to the side for years. If you have lost touch with yourself, dreams can sometimes become a form of entertainment that does not currently produce a feeling of excitement or pleasure.

Chances are, you have been very instrumental in the handiwork of helping others reach their most ambitious goals and helping them to board onto flights of their wildest dreams. Please don't get me wrong, it always feels good to know that you were a part of something greater in the world, so I am not discouraging anyone from being helpful in creating positive memories for other people. Consequently, it's important for you not to take the back seat to accomplishing your own goals and living out your dreams.

Goals don't just get achieved because you have stated it as your goal, and dreams don't just become realized because you have dared yourself to dream. In order to live your best life, YOU have to show up for it. You have to be purposefully taking steps toward the life you want. Realistically, every goal may not be accomplished, and every dream may not be lived out, but you have to start somewhere if you want your life to be more fulfilling. It's like being your own best advocate and agent of change for your life.

It takes planning and effort for the manifestation of the wonderful things we want to get out of life. Goals can be short-term or long-term. They are best achieved when you are the true author of them. Sometimes goals can be hindered or unmet because they were not goals you established for yourself, someone else did! Being honest about your goals is imperative.

Goals can sound good when they are spoken aloud or when they are matched with competition with someone else's goals. If it is not your true desire to accomplish a certain goal, do not waste your time trying to talk yourself into it. It may certainly be a great goal for someone else but putting stress on yourself to appease someone else only dishonors what you want your life to be. Whatever goals you choose to accomplish, write down your steps to getting there so that you will be mindful of what is going to be required of you. This also can be a good strategy to help you evaluate whether your goal is realistic or not.

When you consider the possibility of living out your dreams, it may seem impossible; however, one of the ways to make certain that it *never* materializes is to keep it in your head and *never* engage in any steps or action to explore the possibilities.

Intentional Goal Setting Worksheet

Try playing some soft relaxing music and reserve 30 minutes of your time to complete this exercise for each goal. As you identify your goals, try guesstimating what obstacles are likely to get you off track from accomplishing them, then choose the best course of action you can take to prevent you from being unsuccessful.

MY GOALS
1.
2.
3.
4.
5.

Follow this outline for each goal.

Goal #1:
- Steps required:

- Projected completion date:

- Obstacles likely to get in my way:

- Safeguards I can activate to ensure my success:

Intentional Abundant Life Dream Worksheet

While some dreams may seem impossible, not all of them are! Some dreams are at our fingertips and only a footstep away. These dreams may have never been tapped into at all, even if only to explore the possibility of being lived out on some level. All it takes is your vision and your willingness to move into a posture of readiness!

Dare to Dream Accountability Checkpoint

Abundant Life Dream:

I can see myself wearing, doing, and feeling:

I can see myself living out my dream by this time frame:

One action I can take this week to further explore the possibility:

One action I can take this month to get me closer to my dream or that will allow me to live out my dream:

I can reimagine my dream on a different level and still be happy by doing:

Intentionally Spending Time With People You Enjoy

Can we be real with each other for just a moment! You will not always enjoy the company of some of the people that you socialize with on a regular basis. I realize that there are times and situations in which you may be required to interact with other people for certain social events, religious events, or work-related functions. When I speak of intentionality in this case, I am referring to you making it a priority to frequently spend time with people you can laugh with, who are positive, you share similar interests with, you are able to communicate with openly and honestly, and people who understand you and likewise. I know this description can seem like a tall order, but time is precious.

Consider the time that you may be required to spend with people who you don't necessarily enjoy their company in instances where you may work together or even at family functions. There are 24 hours in a day. A good amount of your 24 hours could easily be reduced by 2 – 10 hours on a given day when you are intentional about the time you spend with others. Meaning, time when you are not required to interact with people who are not your favorites.

Make your precious hours count by selecting and carving out time to socialize with people that you look forward to seeing, being with and speaking to. It is ok for you to choose how you want to spend your leisure time and with whom you want to spend it.

It is important to regularly include social connections as a healthy outlet to balance the stress that naturally comes with routine demands on your time. If you are trying to manage a relationship, parenting responsibilities, and a career you may not even feel like you have time for the people that you really do like, so it may require that you take some time to review your calendar to check for possible availability. In certain instances, more is not always better. You may not have the availability to carve out large amounts of time to socialize but taking some time is better than none at all.

If you are a mother, consider hiring a babysitter or nanny. This is a good option if you do not have family members or friends who can step in to allow you some well-deserved time to socialize, or to have some "me time" to do what will help to fill your cup. If you are a caregiver, consider hiring a home health aide or respite care worker, if you do not have family members or people that you trust to care for your loved one. This can also give you a well-deserved break to recharge. Whether you are a mother or a caregiver, having the help of a housekeeper, even occasionally can make your plate lighter.

Although the pandemic re-shaped certain aspects of social life as we know it today, if you are not completely comfortable with the idea of physically sharing space with others, there are still ways to creatively and safely spend time together. Ways to connect can range from zoom chat lunches, zoom game nights, zoom social mixers, outside dining options to inside limited options while being socially distanced.

You may still feel more comfortable wearing masks at certain social gatherings while others may not choose to wear them. My whole point is that you may only have an hour to spare or may have to deal with various limitations due to several reasons, but if these are people you value then you may be motivated to make the time and tolerate some adjustments in order to enjoy their company.

Take some time to reflect on the people who add value to your life and write it down in the space below. Review your calendar from time to time to look for opportunities to socialize with them.

People I Enjoy Spending Time With	The Last Time We Socialized Was
1.	
2.	
3.	
4.	
5.	
6.	
7.	
8.	

live
laugh
love

CHAPTER THREE

THE SKY IS NOT FALLING; YOU JUST NEED TO RELAX

RELAXATION SHOULD NOT BE A BACK UP PLAN

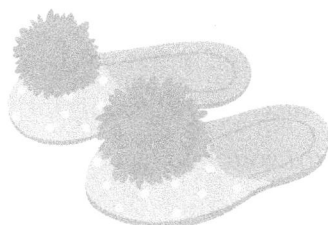

While relaxation is one of the most valuable tools for managing stress, it is not given the time or credit it deserves. It is often the most neglected forms of self-care in women. You may have only utilized the word "relaxation" to describe what you would like to be able to do at some point. You may already be feeling so overwhelmed by life that just thinking about taking the time to relax stresses you out. Unfortunately, when relaxation is left out of the regimen of your life, so is your peace. Women tend to prioritize other people and other obligations over recharging themselves. Sydney J. Harris, an American Journalist sounds the alarm with this quote: "The time to relax is when you don't have time for it."

Your stress response has a way of coming out during times you least expect it to. You may not even realize it when you are being snappy or lashing out at someone about something very trivial. If that person does not bring it to your attention, this could develop into a pattern of behavior that continues and could possibly affect your relationship with them in a negative way. As stress mounts up, there is an even greater need for relaxation. If you have been told "you need to relax" "you need a vacation", or "girl, chill out", then it is highly evident that others are aware that you are stressed.

I am making such a big deal out of the need for relaxation because, IT IS A BIG DEAL! Since stress is the leading cause of mental problems and physical problems, it behooves us all to surrender to a lifestyle of relaxation. Relaxation can be described as the state of being free from tension and anxiety. It decreases the effects of stress on your mind and body. It's also a wonderful way to reward your body and mind for all the emotional and physical strain that has been endured. Furthermore, there are endless and significant benefits to relaxing. Familiarize yourself with some of the perks you can expect to gain when you make room for relaxation.

- Lowering blood pressure

- Slowing your heart rate

- Improving Indigestion

- Maintaining normal blood sugar levels

- Improving sleep quality

- Reducing muscle tension and chronic pain

- Reducing activity of stress hormones

- Increasing blood flow to major muscles

- Reducing anger and frustration

- Boosting confidence to handle problems

- Improving concentration and mood

- Improving function of the immune system (or strengthening the immune system)

Relaxation is simply the gift that keeps on giving! Trust me, with all of those benefits you will not be on the losing hand. As women, we are prone to encountering more of the mental and physical aspects of stress. Genetics also play a big factor into certain conditions that women may experience. For example, according to a report from the Office of Minority Health, African American women are 60 percent more likely to have high blood pressure, as compared to non-hispanic white women. As an African American woman, that report is alarming to me.

As women in general, we tend to bear the majority, if not all of the burden when it comes down to caregiving responsibilities at home while trying to balance work and personal life activities, so we must be more intentional about making time to focus on our emotional and physical well-being.

Give Yourself the Gift of Relaxation

The time needed for relaxation can vary from person to person and the form of relaxation can vary as well. Impactful relaxation can range from just a few minutes to several hours.

There are many ways to relax, just like there are different ways to style your hair. Choosing how to relax depends upon what activities you get the most benefit from mentally and physically. Some women may prefer activities that require physical exertion while others may prefer activities that require very little movement. Some women may find cooking very relaxing to them, while others may find it very stressful. Remember, this is about what helps you relax. If you have not given any thought about ways to relax, I would like to share a few with you. Review the suggestions below to find and re-experience your "happy place" again and again!

RELAXANITAS (relaxation that can occur in 5 minutes or less)

4-7-8 Breathing Technique: It allows your body to enter a deep state of relaxation relatively quickly. It's really simple: First, empty out the air from your lungs. Next, with your mouth closed, breathe in quietly through your nose as you count in your head for 4 seconds. Then for seven seconds, hold your breath. Lastly, exhale from your mouth forcefully pursing your lips making a whooshing sound. Keeping the tip of your tongue rested against the roof of your mouth throughout this technique helps to make the whooshing sound. Dr. Andrew Weil recommends practicing this technique every day, twice a day for starters; subsequently, you can use it to reduce anxiety and even manage food cravings. Whenever anything upsetting happens, this technique can prevent you from reacting. An additional benefit of this technique is that it helps you fall asleep at bedtime. Repeat the cycle of breathing for 4 times.

Candle Gazing Mindfulness Meditation: Light a candle. Take three deep breaths and watch the flame dance. Whatever comes to your mind, notice it, let it pass on by like clouds in the sky does and then refocus your attention back to the flame.

Herbal Tea Meltdown: Drink a cup of your favorite herbal tea and let your worries melt away. Notice the aroma and flavor of the tea while enjoying each sip.

Journaling Jewel: Unclutter your mind by emptying onto paper any worries, negative thoughts, or feelings. Releasing your emotional pain is much healthier than stuffing your pain. Besides, when you empty out your concerns and worries on paper, they no longer have the need to rent space in your head.

Musical Miracle: Listen to soft relaxing music that quiets your mind, calms your body, and eases stress or listen to upbeat music that motivates you to move (get your dance on), it can help you feel more optimistic about life.

Pet Therapy Pickup: Hug or cuddle with your pet. Fur babies offer unconditional love and companionship. They are always excited to receive and give affection.

Paramount Prayer: Voice any concerns and needs that you have. Don't be afraid to be vulnerable. This is your dedicated time to release your burdens and make requests for divine intervention on your behalf. Connection with God's presence equals power!

Praise Party: What a great way to start out your day by celebrating! You are alive! Simply reflect on all of the wonderful blessings in your life despite the challenges you have faced. It's almost like gratitude on steroids! Experience the joy and give thanks again and again!

Serenity Shower: Enjoy a warm shower, meditate on the word, C-A-L-M or any word that ushers in the presence of tranquility, while the water gently beats against your skin and washes away your worries. This is a good time to add a little aromatherapy by using shower steamers infused with relaxing essential oils.

RELAXATUDES (relaxation mindset and movement that occurs within 1 hour or less)

Blissful Bubble Bath: Fill your bathtub with warm water, bath salts, bath bombs, a few drops of essential oils, or fragranced bubble bath liquid. Make it the ultimate bath experience by adding soft music, fragrant candles, or your favorite cool drink.

Mood Mending Massage: As the tension leaves your muscles, your mind can now focus on taking in peace, well-being, and gratitude. You can put your cares on pause to allow a peaceful transition from stress and worry to relaxation, calm, ease, and relief.

Reading Release: Decompress by reading books that help you to unwind and disconnect from technology. Read something light, spiritual, encouraging, or comical to balance out the stressors from your day.

Television Tickle: Treat yourself to a funny sitcom or comedy show to add some humor in your day. Between work, parental responsibilities, household tasks, financial concerns, and relationship issues, taking a break to recalibrate your stressors and laughing out loud may be just what the doctor ordered. After all, laughter is like medicine to the soul!

Wonderment Walk: Take a walk being totally mindful of the positive things and people you have in your life. This could be a stroll on the beach or more active walking. Enjoy walking and tapping into the amazement of how your body just keeps working for you without you having to tell it to do anything. You can even bring your pet along for added enjoyment. Notice the flowers, clouds, rainbows, people, sunrises, sunsets, birds, and waterfalls. Notice the gentle breeze, the crisp cool air, or the warm sun on your skin. Notice sounds and fragrances.

Yes, to Yoga: Answer the call to receiving a mind-body-spirit balance. With each pose, breathing technique, or guided meditation, your brain and body is rejuvenated. You are much better equipped to take on the demands of your day. Just imagine having a nice well-balanced tune up! Namaste!

THE SKY IS NOT FALLING; YOU JUST NEED TO RELAX

RELAXULTIMATES: (A Relaxation supreme experience that occurs in a couple of hours to a couple of weeks)

Spa Splurge: Pamper yourself with a smorgasbord of delightful, and breath-taking self-care practices such as a full body massage, facial, mud wrap, waxing, foot bath, pedicure, manicure, and aromatherapy. Select a couple of these soothing treasures to begin or end your day in a relaxed posture. Not only will you gain the benefit of relaxation, but also improvement in your circulation, reduction of inflammation, and the restoration of your mind and body. Spending just a few hours nurturing yourself can make a big difference in your day, week and even in your relationships.

One Day Relaxing Getaway: Indulgence without a huge expense or suitcase! You get an opportunity to escape within a two-to-three-hour drive. You can recharge yourself by going to the beach, taking a river boat cruise, going to a state or national park, visiting a botanical garden, picnic, museum, or aquarium. For an added benefit you can create new and beautiful memories by inviting family members, friends, or your significant other.

Soothing Staycation: Create your own relaxing environment in your home or take a brief walk into your backyard to connect with nature by setting up a tent for camping. Consider escaping from the hustle and bustle of life to a nearby town or city that is known for its quiet and simple lifestyle. You can even spoil yourself overnight at a local resort while enjoying the amenities to the utmost. Have a sip of your favorite beverage, take a warm and soothing bath, listen to soft and relaxing music, enjoy room service for dinner, relax in the whirlpool or go for a swim. Since it's all about YOU, you can choose to just lounge around in your robe and watch tv or read what interests you until your heart is content. Resist the temptation to work or to focus on anyone else during this time. Remember, work will always be there waiting for your return so make the best of your break away from it!

Mini Vacation: Maximize your time off from work with a brief intermission from life's hectic moments. Kick back and detach from the to do lists by taking a three or four-day weekend to unwind. Try renting an Airbnb, cabin in the mountains, going on a short cruise, renting a beach house, or attending a women's retreat. You can also make it a family trip or a girl's trip. Consider extending a business trip to accommodate for some well-deserved "me time." What a great way to achieve work-personal life balance!

It doesn't have to stop here! Of course, if you can take a longer vacation do not deprive yourself of doing so. Reward yourself with a week or more of immeasurable ways to relax and be pampered. Visiting local hide-a-ways, famous landmarks, tropical islands, or venturing out of the country to the most peaceful destinations can all be delightful ways for you to release stress, reset your mind, and recharge your personal battery. Indulge in a healthy dose of self-care by creatively and lovingly crafting the epitome of a vacation by incorporating several of the above-mentioned forms of relaxation.

My Relaxation Commitment Plan

Once a day, I will take time to relax by:

Once a week, I will pamper myself by:

Once a year, I will reward myself by:

it's
TIME
- TO -
Relax

CHAPTER FOUR

EMPTY CALORIES WHILE DOING IT YOUR WAY

EMBRACE EXERCISE

S ome say milk does the body good, well I say, exercise does the body even better! I know there are valid reasons why some women cannot exercise such as an illness or injury. However, there are some of you who already have a built-in excuse just waiting! This chapter is the shortest chapter in the book, not because it's not valuable but because I am not an expert in exercise and physical fitness; however, I have learned some things that currently benefit me in my journey to well-being as far as exercise goes.

Let's be clear, no one particular exercise program will fit every woman's needs. With different builds, ages, health challenges, and personal interests, exercise works best when it is tailor made for you. In Chapter One you learned how stress can affect you mentally and physically. The 4 M's of Mental Health (*mindfulness, **movement**, meaning, and mastery*) are recommended for dealing with stress, anxiety, and depression. Since we are focusing on exercise in this chapter, understanding the value of movement in your daily life is very important. Getting regular healthy movement in your lifestyle can be a game changer on so many levels for your overall well-being. According to the CDC, (Physical Activity Guidelines for Americans, 2nd Edition) - cdc.gov August 2020, A single bout of moderate-to-vigorous physical activity provides immediate benefits to your health and regular physical activity provides important health benefits for chronic disease prevention. For example, some immediate returns on investment, you can experience is improvement in sleep, reduced feelings of anxiety and reduced blood pressure. Some long-term paybacks include reduced risk of developing dementia, alzheimer's, depression, reduced risk for heart disease, stroke, type 2 diabetes, lowered risk of several cancers, reduced risks of falls, improved bone health, and reduced risk of weight gain. You have been learning how to combat stress mentally and emotionally, now it's time to get physical! I would like to add at this point, it is strongly recommended to consult with your physician prior to starting your workout. Before we dive into getting you moving, let's talk about a few things that are important to consider when exploring your exercise type.

What are your goals? Many women exercise to lose weight while others prefer endurance. If you are exercising to lose weight, it is a good idea to identify how much weight you would like to lose. Exercises that are more geared toward weight loss are walking, cycling, Pilates, swimming, running/jogging, yoga, weight training and interval training. Endurance workouts are activities that increase your breathing and heart rate. Some examples of these workouts include walking, jogging, swimming, biking, and jumping rope. (www.heart.org.fitness-basics). Your focus could be strength training, or you could be performance driven. If your target is to strengthen your muscles, this will allow you the ability to perform everyday activities and protect your body from injuries. Here is another tip, stronger muscles help you burn more calories even when your body is at rest. Hmmmmm....that definitely works for me. (www.heart.org.fitness-basics). On the other hand, performance training is simply designed to improve your fitness level for the purpose of improving your ability to perform a given sport. As said earlier, being physically active is good for your overall health, but choosing the best activities for your goals will help you to achieve your goals.

What do you enjoy? Certain exercises can be challenging but they can also be enjoyable and leaving you energized. Depending on the exercise or movement you incorporate in your workout, it can actually be a lot of fun. Working out at a gym will allow you to get out of the house and socialize with others. For example, group workouts at the gym may not only be fun, but can be motivating for each other.

Jazzercise, Zumba, Line dancing are all entertaining ways to enjoy breaking a little sweat! Since we are talking about motivation, some people find that retaining a personal trainer for an individual workout may help them to stay on track and perform the exercises correctly to avoid injuries. Perhaps working out alone may be your preference and that is ok, because at the end of the day, rewind and repeat again, it's all about Y-O-U!

It's also important to explore what format you prefer. You may find that the gym is intimidating, too far away, or too costly, but do not allow that to prevent you from getting some movement. Another option is to consider doing your workout at home. Using your home as a workout space could help you save money and time. You may feel more comfortable as you work away those calories in the comfort of your own home while having more flexibility. Remember, exercise is a good way of taking care of you so that you can be around a lot longer.

What equipment do you need? At most gyms, the equipment you need will probably already be there. Working out at home may require you to gather or purchase your equipment prior to beginning your workout. Preparing ahead of time helps you to be successful in meeting your goals and it also takes away your excuse for not having everything you need. Some common workout equipment for home is resistance bands, weights, pcv pipe, yoga/pilates ball, mats, door pulley.

Are you preparing your body with the fuel needed to reach your goals? As we grow older, our bodies change and therefore have different requirements. One of the changes specifically is nutrition. It is important to develop a healthy eating plan to fuel your body adequately as you work out. You may need to seek out a Nutritionist or Dietician to gain guidance as to what is appropriate for you.

Drinking lots of water is a necessary part of this equation as well. When you exercise, sweat is released through your skin, and you lose body fluid. Drinking water during exercise helps to replenish the fluids that you lose when you exercise. But to be honest with you, whether you exercise or not, drinking water regularly should be incorporated into your daily routine. While there are many benefits to drinking water, a few of them happen to be: decreased constipation, prevention of urinary tract and bladder infections, decreased risk of kidney stones, and skin hydration according to healthline (healthline.com). The most significant factor in addition to the above list, is that we need water to survive! Although, we've been told that the recommended daily intake of water is eight 8-ounce glasses a day, there are other differing opinions that base adequate water intake on weight, age, and gender.

Set yourself up for success! When planning your workout schedule, it is so important to be committed. So, in other words, do not set a goal that you are unlikely to reach, and you already know it. Establish realistic goals for yourself. Your workout goals should not be compared to anyone else's. There are simply too many variables to take into consideration when it comes down to why something works for someone else but not for you! The list is way too long to mention.

If you find that you are overwhelmed by your goal once you begin your workout, it is ok to adjust it to a goal that is more attainable for you. I find that upbeat music helps me to get through my workouts while I am moving to the beats. I would also recommend being kind to yourself as you begin to work toward your goals. Sticking to anything can be challenging for many people. For every day that you complete a workout, give yourself a compliment like, "girl, that was a great workout today" or "great job, you did it." If you did not reach the goal that you wanted to that day, use kind words of encouragement toward yourself like, " it's ok, tomorrow will be a better day" or "doing some physical activity is better than doing no physical activity."

Crews Nugget #2: Remember, you can never fail at anything if you keep trying.

My Workout Commitment Plan

1) Exercises or movements I feel most comfortable doing is:

2) I will engage in these exercises or movements _____ days a week.

3) Motivational song I will listen to motivate me is:

4) Positive self-talk I will use to motivate me is:

Chapter Five

CHANGE YOUR APPETITE FOR STRESS

SET REALISTIC EXPECTATIONS OF YOURSELF

Y ou may not even realize that you have acquired a taste for stress. Now I do get it, some stress is inevitable. I am not suggesting at all that you are on the prowl for stress, but I am saying that you may be more vulnerable to stress depending on your daily life practices.

There are some beliefs, habits, or behaviors that make some women more susceptible to stress than others. Buckle up ladies and prepare for the ride! Come along with me on this thought - provoking journey to explore if and how you may be creating or adding to your stress.

Think about all the things that are on your plate currently. Some tasks are on your plate that are necessary, but some are not. Whether you are single or married, with or without children, there will always be something more to do. There comes a time when enough must simply be enough!

If you are already aware that you have been doing the same thing but expecting different results, I am encouraging you to please stop making investments in perpetuating your own stress! In this chapter, I will take a moment to address women in different statuses and how you can develop a healthier appetite to overcome stress. You will also learn how to be more comfortable letting go of things that don't serve you well, how to embrace not having certain things on your plate and how to prioritize things that are on your plate.

"It is also equally important to avoid measuring your progress using someone else's ruler" (SIBCareerCoaching.Com). When was the last time you just allowed yourself to be you! I mean, the real you! Not comparing yourself to any other women at all. Maybe you can't even remember a time when you didn't look at another woman to judge yourself.

You may be thinking about how well the superwoman working next you is getting things done with such ease, a smile on her face, and a trim body too. Perhaps, you may be wondering how other women have been able to launch their businesses, write books, secure promotions, enjoy a home cooked meal almost every day, have a clean home, work on an advanced degree, engage in fun activities with their kids, take vacations regularly and keep an active love life too.

You may also be convinced that you must be doing something wrong! Because after all, if other women can do all of this stuff and then some, you should also be able to accomplish those things too right? What do other women have that you don't, you may be asking yourself? Simply put, all women are not created equal and that is ok!

I was having a session with a client via zoom and I noticed that she kept looking in a different direction and appearing very frustrated as she was typing. I asked her what she was doing, and she replied that she was trying to manage three zoom meetings at one time. She was attempting to navigate her therapy session, a work meeting, and a planning session for her sorority. I began to feel overwhelmed just by watching her try to work her superwoman magic. I gave her the option to reschedule her therapy appointment to a date and time when she could actually be present in the session and devote uninterrupted time to her emotional well-being.

Ladies, even though the zoom platform has created the illusion that you can be many places at the same time, from a mental health standpoint, that is alarming to me, why you would attempt to do so. Your physical body can only be in one place at a time, so why should your mind be challenged to share mental space with different venues at the same time.

During my next session, with my client, I made her aware of the importance of blocking off uninterrupted time in her schedule to invest in self-care. I further explained to her that therapy is one of the most rewarding forms of self-care. I also reminded her that being a jack of all trades is not conducive to the mastery of them.

As a therapist, I know that the pressure to look a certain way, feel a certain way, act a certain way, and accomplish certain things can be unbearable to live up to. Please understand that what is perceived as a perfect picture to the human eye, definitely requires a second look with lenses that are more reality based and more self accepting. Truthfully, a second look with different lenses, of course, will allow you to clearly see that the all-encompassing, flawless picture that you have been trying to measure up to is something that simply does not exist for any woman.

Crews Nugget #3: The picture you paint, the brush you choose to paint with, the colors you select, the number of strokes and the canvas you utilize will become your creation. That means that your picture doesn't have to look like someone else's for it to be beautiful and impactful.

Your Shoes are Made for Your Journey

Anyone who knows me personally, knows of my deep affection for shoes. I love the different styles, textures, colors, and brands of shoes. Some women prefer flats, while others prefer high heels. Some prefer sandals while others prefer flip flops. Some prefer sneakers while others prefer boots.

Most women share my love connection with shoes and have a variety of them to prove it. I personally like to try my shoes on and walk around in them for a bit. I am also careful to see how they look on my feet in the mirror. Sometimes, I will even envision certain outfits with the shoes, which further propels my shoe appetite for more of them. Lest I digress.... as I shop for shoes, I often check out the selection of styles that other women are choosing.

It should come as no surprise to you by now that it does not take much to inspire me to purchase a pair or two of shoes, even when I know I don't need them. As I watch other women and think to myself, "hmmm, those look so good on her, maybe I will try that pair too." It is not long before I discover that those shoes do not suit me. Rather it's the pattern, fit, shape, or color, something about them does not sit well enough for me to race to the counter to purchase them.

When it comes down to your pair of shoes, you are the one who should be choosing them because you are the one who will be wearing them. It's quite interesting how we take along our girlfriends on shopping trips and ask their advice for which pair of shoes to buy as if they will be wearing them. William Shakespeare said it best, "to thine own self be true."

On the road of experiential learning, many heartaches are felt, and many mistakes are made. What comes out of the journey is wisdom, confidence, and success. No one can tell you what your experience was like better than you, just like no one can tell you how comfortable or uncomfortable your shoes feel to you better than you can. Your journey was designed just for you in the same way as the shoes you wear.

If you subscribe to what other women are doing and attempt to travel on their journey, you will always come up short because their journey is not meant for you. Do not stress yourself out by trying to replicate something that is not even congruent with who you are. Do not try to borrow anyone else's shoes to conform or fit in because their style will not fit you and you will never be happy trying to experience the same comfort level or appeal that they have. How another woman struts in her shoes has everything to do with HER experience. Your experience when wearing your stilettos speaks volumes so be confident and create your own stroll.

There are specific characteristics about you that make you fit for your journey no matter what anyone else thinks, which means that no one else can travel on your journey nor travel in your shoes. Every woman has unique qualities about themselves that makes them successful in many aspects of their lives. You are the one who defines what success looks like for you!

If the responsibility is left up to others to measure or define what success is for you, frustration, disappointment, resentment, low self-esteem, and discouragement become cyclical in your life. Simply let it go girl, and free yourself from the cravings of a validation elixir. Don't be so generous by inviting undeserved criticism, judgment, or unrealistic expectations of others upon you. This of course, will allow someone else to take away your power, your progress, and your purpose! After all, it's your journey and your shoes are the right fit!

Crews Nugget #4: The finished product of a beautiful painting is often desired by many women, just like a stylish pair of shoes. Always consider the challenges and obstacles another woman may have faced in the midst of creating such a masterpiece of art! High-definition women take pride in their accomplishments and do not need the approval of others. They have learned how to be comfortable in their own skin and in their own pair of shoes!

Stress Appetite Assessment (SAA):

Take a moment to complete this assessment to learn if you may be creating your own stress by establishing unrealistic expectations for yourself or even for others. In other words, you may be setting yourself up for great disappointment. Please check off all that apply to you. Make this a "no judgment" assessment. This tool is all about awareness and growth!

- I place things on my plate to do even though I know I will not have time to complete them.

- I voluntarily obligate myself to do things for others to avoid feeling guilty or to alleviate their stress.

- I constantly procrastinate on doing things until the last minute.

- I compare myself to others, even though others' circumstances are different from mine.

- I expect that I will be shown the same level of kindness that I show to others.

- I expect people to like me because I am a nice person.

- I expect to get a promotion on my job because I am often the last one to leave work.

- I am not good enough if others don't accept me.

- I must do things a certain way or I won't be happy.

- If I don't complete a goal or an important task, then I am a failure.

- I expect others to agree with my viewpoint.

- I expect others to know what I want or need.

- I expect others to make me happy.

- I should be making seven figures by now.

- I should have known how to (help, stop, save) him or her.

- I can change him or her, it may just take some more time.

- If I don't have children or am not married by a certain time frame, then something is wrong with me.

- I rarely take vacations because it shows how dedicated I am to my role at home or work.

- I constantly worry about things that are outside of my control.

It's OK to Be a Woman of Expectancy (WOE)

Women of Expectancy can be used to describe any woman that may be waiting for your mate or waiting for your bundle of joy at some point in your life. It can be anything that you have been hoping or praying for but just have not received it YET! It may be your desire to have one or more of these components in your life, but do you have time to share emotional and personal space with anyone else right now?

Whatever you have been hoping or praying for, if you received it right now, how would it be positioned in your life? I recommend that you take an inventory to identify things on your plate that may need to be removed from your plate. You may need to check for any time-wasting activities. Sometimes the busyness of life can prevent you from possessing the things you really want in your life. Explore what your busyness is about and if it is serving you well.

Make sure that you are getting a good return on investment of your time and energy in people and activities. For instance, are you placing your energy in hopeless situations with partners who are not physically and emotionally available to you? If this is your situation, you are likely to find yourself constantly being stressed, frustrated, and disappointed. You may even be questioning whether you are good enough or not.

Suppose your special someone is in your life already and you are just very eager to become a mother. Could you be placing so much of your focus on becoming a mother that you are missing out on what is lovely in your life right now. Examining what goals you want to accomplish prior to kids or marriage can be very cathartic. Searching for the perfect career or mate; achieving the perfect body size or bank account may be keeping you stuck and feeling inadequate.

Placing your energy in people and activities that do not add value to your life can often leave you feeling disappointed. There is a familiar saying that "good things come to those who wait." There is nothing wrong with having expectations but just make sure you are giving yourself permission to be happy while you wait!

Tips for Your Journey

- Consider taking a Mental Health Day - Although I do recommend taking vacations when you can, giving yourself a mental recharge in between can help you be more productive and feel less overwhelmed. Recharging mentally can be accomplished by doing absolutely nothing or engaging in some well overdue self-care. Refer back to Chapter Three for more ways to take full advantage of your day off.

- Give yourself permission to ask for and accept help. No one can do everything alone and even if there are things that you can do without the help of others, it doesn't mean that you should. Simply allow yourself to enjoy someone else's attention being directed toward YOU for a change! Asking for help is a strength, not a weakness.

- Remove some things off your plate that either demand too much of your time or that are not fulfilling, then replace them with activities that you find more pleasurable.

- Shift your priorities – Everything and everyone else can't be your priority. Some things and some people just have to wait! It may be uncomfortable for them and you, but that's ok!

- Stop focusing on what others around you are doing and be the action that you are waiting to see in others.

- While you are waiting for your well-deserved promotion or better job opportunity to come along, take career development classes.

- Say goodbye to lifeless and energy sucking relationships.

- Stop waiting for the perfect time, mate, career, or body size before you allow yourself to be happy. Choose to be happy NOW!

Steps of Women of Resilience (WOR)

Women of Resilience can be used to describe women who have been on the journey to emotional, relational, and spiritual wellness for a while, even though the scars are not always visible. You kept marching regardless of the pace or the obstacles. You may have children and are ok with not being married, you may be married but do not have any children and you are ok with that, or you may not be seeking a relationship and unable to have children and have made peace with that as well.

Your career or finances may not be exactly where you want them to be at this time. In fact, you may have even gotten passed over for several promotions and asked to train the person(s) being hired for the promotion. The Oxford English Dictionary defines resilience as the capacity to withstand or recover quickly from difficulties. This definition tells me that the many challenges faced over time broke you down sometimes, humbled you, but indeed grew you. Your setback was a setup for the win! This is what makes your lemonade story so refreshing!

Sometimes the things that we don't have are a blessing to us. Women of Resilience have recognized this, wrote the book on it, and are prepared to read it to others if needed. Having people and things in our lives comes with responsibility. Sometimes the responsibility may be so overwhelming that you may not be able to enjoy having that person or thing in your life. For example, being in a relationship can be wonderful, if you are with the right person. However, if you happen to be with someone who makes you cry way more than they make you smile or laugh, then chances are you would be just fine without that person taking up time and space in your life.

I remember many years ago, I applied for a job that I felt I was qualified for. I was so excited about the opportunity to interview for the job, and I thought that the interview had gone well. I received a phone call from the hiring director letting me know that although they were impressed by my interview and skills, they decided to go with a different applicant. Of course, I felt very disappointed. A few months later, I was speaking to a colleague of mine, who told me, that particular company reorganized and the department that I applied for was eliminated. Now I don't have to tell you how thankful I was for not getting that job!

Having resilience does not mean that you have things all figured out or that you won't face difficulties and disappointments. It also does not mean that you don't desire more out of life. Instead, it means that despite adversity, hardship, tragedy, and sorrow....... you have learned the rhythm of movement in your life. Yes, the journey can be lonely at times, overwhelming, the children can test you beyond measure, and your finances can be a mystery puzzle, but you know what it takes to navigate to your destiny because you are a survivor!

Tips for Your Journey:

- Honor every step of your journey by giving yourself love, compassion, and even forgiveness.

- Celebrate your victories, you earned them! This is the time to look at yourself in the mirror and say, "Girl, you are the cake, the icing and the sprinkles on top."

- Take some time to relax and reward yourself with scheduled days of pampering. Refer back to Chapter Three for more ways to take full advantage of "me time."

- Don't stop dreaming even in the midst of your peace! Peace is priceless but so is life. You can enjoy both at the same time. Identify some things that you were not able to accomplish but would still like to.

- Write a list of 3 things you hoped or prayed for but did not get them. Then write down how not having those things was for your own good. Here is where you take a victory lap ladies!

- Know your worth! In relationships, careers, and all aspects of life, understand that you matter! You did not get this far in life by not being of value to others.

- Please tell your story again and again about how you got over! Share what helped you to keep moving. So many younger women need your voice of wisdom. They need to know that it wasn't easy, but it was possible! You can do this in women's groups, retreats, support groups, etc.

- Consider writing a book about your journey. One of the best ways to ensure that you never forget your struggle and that others can learn from your struggle is to put it in writing.

Crews Nugget #5: Know who you are and wear it well! You do not have to be ashamed of who you are or what you have been through. There are many parts that make up who you are. Love all parts of you, even the parts that you feel are not so flattering.

End Your Relationship With the Peace Robber

Peace is priceless! So why do so many of us women allow our peace to be disturbed so often? We have to do a better job at being more protective of our peace. I will be the first to admit that there are many things in the world today that are very unsettling and tough to stomach. When situations occur that give us concern, we tend to worry about the outcomes of those situations.

Worrying, also known as overthinking, is a state of mind that allows one to dwell on difficulties or problems. These situations can include health challenges, finances, job stressors, relationships issues, world violence and tragedy, politics, etc. Worry is a common emotion that comes up when you feel uncertain about the future. I will cut you some slack here because occasional worry is a normal part of life; however, chronic or excessive worry can lead to increased anxiety which can morph into more problematic anxiety disorders. It can interfere greatly with everyday functioning and affect your eating habits, sleep pattern, relationships and job performance.

Worrying can also lead to health conditions such as stomach ulcers, chronic pain, strokes, and heart disease. When worrying takes control of your state of mind, it not only robs you of your peace but uncomfortable physical symptoms such as nausea, diarrhea, headaches, and heart palpitations prevent you from being able to get your bearings. You may also notice being restless, edgy, or jumpy. With all of these physical vibes going on it is needless to say that being able to concentrate on anything at this point is nearly impossible.

When is the last time you found yourself sitting up at night or lying in bed staring up at your ceiling? Chances are that you might be worrying about something that you have not had an opportunity to process. Since some worrying is normal, it is best for us to focus on how to manage unnecessary or excessive worry that leads to stress and anxiety disorders. Did you know that it is said that 90% of things that people worry about never even happens? As your wrap your mind around that assessment, consider the huge amount of time and energy devoted to something that the odds are stacked up so heavily against it not occurring!

When trying to manage worry, it is important to pinpoint what it is that you are worried about. Sometimes it may not be so easy to clearly identify what the object of your worry is. Emptying out your brain on paper is a good way to start to sort out what worries may be on your mind. In cases where worries stem from the anticipation of future outcomes, it is beneficial to bring that runaway train to a halt.

There is sometimes the fear that something bad is going to happen which tends to sound the alarm for anxiety or panic. The fear of the unknown and "what if's" seem to do a number on any sense of serenity. We can manage these worries and fears by seeing them through to the end or disrupt them quickly so that they no longer rent space in her minds. On the next few pages, you will learn strategies to help you do both.

But What If This Happens???

In the space below, record what you are worried about or fearful that it will happen. Next, ask yourself if it is possible for something else to occur about your situation on a more positive level. Then directly below it, record what would happen if that bad outcome or worst-case scenario did not occur. Switch gears and imagine if there is a more positive outcome possible. If your brain can entertain the worst-case scenario, then it is also possible for it to entertain other alternatives that are positive. Lastly, allow your mind to focus on that positive emotion. I have included an example to help you get started.

But what if this happens?: *I'm worried that the doctor is going to give me really bad news about my test results when I see her next week.*

Is it possible for something else to occur on a more positive level? *Yes*

What could that something else be with a more positive outcome? *The doctor could tell me that I have a clean bill of health and I don't have anything to worry about.*

How would that feel to me? *That would feel great and I would be able to relax and move on with my life.*

NOW IT'S YOUR TURN!!!

But What If This Happens???

In the space below, record what you are worried about or fearful that it will happen. Next, ask yourself if it is possible for something else to occur about your situation on a more positive level. Then directly below it, record what would happen if that bad outcome or worst-case scenario did not occur. Switch gears and imagine if there is a more positive outcome possible. If your brain can entertain the worst-case scenario, then it is also possible for it to entertain other alternatives that are positive. Lastly, allow your mind to focus on that positive emotion.

But what if this happens?

Is it possible for something else to occur on a more positive level?

What could that something else be with a more positive outcome?

How would that feel to me?

Don't Always Believe the Stories That Your Mind Creates

Life can throw some really tough and fast curve balls that make us question why certain things happened. This type of questioning, although it is normal, can sometimes send out the search team in our mind's eye to try to find solutions or answers to make sense of why a situation occurred. When the question is posed, it completely takes over the brain's thought process.

Sometimes in the search for answers, stories/false narratives can be created that become intertwined with reality, especially when a high level of stress, anxiety or trauma is involved. The information or answers certainly feel real enough. The line between imaginations/perceptions and reality are not always so clear.

When the brain is stuck on something that may not be based on reality, it can be challenging for it to become unstuck and transition into reality-based thinking without strategies or techniques to get the translation of certain narratives back on track. For instance, you may be convinced that you are on the brink of losing your position at work because there were actually some layoffs in a different department. This interpretation or assumption heightens your anxiety, although your boss told you that you were doing a great job and your department would not be facing any layoffs.

While you were at lunch, you saw your boss speaking with the CFO of the company. The reality of the situation is the knowledge of layoffs in another department, your boss's reassurance that your department was safe, and you observing your boss and the CFO of your company speaking with each other. That is what you know to be true at this point.

Now this is where things start to go offline and the narrative begins to change. You interpret that that your boss and the CFO were discussing layoffs in your department that also include you. Of course, you begin to connect dots that do not necessarily go together without any supporting proof or evidence. Subsequently, this interpretation of what you observed and perceived to be your reality has caused you to suffer from trouble sleeping, nightmares, nervousness, headaches, chest palpitations, and nausea. A quick dose of reality is warranted here by far!

My forever go to is to stop and take a deep cleansing breath. Then take a step back to give yourself some safe emotional distance from the situation by utilizing a strategy that I call "My Day in Court." In this strategy, you would imagine yourself being in a courtroom with the task of presenting proof or evidence of your claim. In this case, you would need to identify the proof or evidence that you **will** be laid off. Let me say here that no one knows the future and what is before you at this moment can always change. However, we cannot live life predicting our future by connecting dots that do not have any basis for being connected in the present. So I imagine you would feel like what you believe is real but I would have to say, what proof would you be able to present to the judge to win your case?

If you have ever watched court television or attended court in person, then you probably already know that if evidence or proof is not provided to the Judge to substantiate your claim, then it is usually kicked out of court or dismissed. Likewise, assumptions, and interpretations, no matter how real they feel must be kicked out of your mind and dismissed or disputed so that you can let go of the anxiety and get back to your daily life activities.

The use of reality testing as a technique allows you to assess a situation for what it really is, rather than what you hope or fear it might be. This technique is also used to adjust perceptions that do not conform to the realities of the situation. On the next page, write down whatever it is that you may be convincing yourself to believe. Then write down the PROOF or EVIDENCE that you have in order to support that belief or narrative.

Keep in mind it may be hard to resist the temptation to write down information that you think may have connections that could lead to the evidence, but if you do not have the evidence or proof, then your case would be dismissed. You are not being dismissed but your case is! Don't waste any more of your time trying to connect dots, instead, do something fun or relaxing! You can also tell yourself until there is proof and something to be worried about, you will not focus on anything that is not in the present.

My Day In Court

The situation that I am worried about is:

What is my belief about the situation or what am I telling myself about the situation?

The proof or evidence that I have to support my belief is?

If there is no proof or evidence, what can I do or tell myself so that I can release myself from unnecessary worry and anxiety?

Schedule Your Worry Time

Women are always so busy, and our calendars seem to be packed with numerous events and deadlines to meet. I am sure that most women, if not all, are not sitting around waiting for the next best thing or issue to worry about. There seems to be more on our minds than we know what to do with.

Women are prone to remember details. The more details we have in our minds, the more we seem to worry. As a matter of fact, during my graduate studies, I was told that women's brains were compared to a bowl of spaghetti because our brains are very active, and every thought and issue is connected to another in some way. This connectivity is said to allow women to make quick transitions such as multi-tasking and be better at social skills. On the other hand, a man's brain was described more like cabinet drawers that can only be pulled out one at a time.

When distressing thoughts cross our minds about different situations and events, it can be easy to drift off into worry land even in the most inconvenient times. Why not set aside time to worry about these issues when it is less likely to interfere with your goals or social activities. I know this concept probably seems a bit impossible, however, it can be done. Choose a time during the day in which you can devote 15 minutes to "worry" about concerns you may have. Schedule your worry time at the same time everyday. Set a timer so that you do not spend any more time worrying than you should. During your worry time, you can choose to write down your worries or just think about them. When your timer goes off, simply end your worry time. You can also use the time to brainstorm for solutions. If you have written your concerns onto paper or process them in your mind, once the timer goes off, put your paper away and consider your job done for the day knowing that you will have another opportunity to go at it again tomorrow.

Once you process your worries in your mind, then tell yourself that you have fulfilled your task and now it is time to put your worries away on the top shelf in an imaginary closet leaving the door closed. Tomorrow awaits you if you are still feeling the need to pick up where you left off. I know it may seem like 15 minutes is not enough but trust me it is! On the next day, begin your worry practice again for 15 minutes until you reach a point of feeling like there is nothing left to worry about, or you don't have the need to worry.

I recommend choosing a time in the morning before you go to work or before you begin your routine activities. You may even choose to use your worry time during your shower. The purpose of tackling your worries first, is because you can get them off your mind early enough in the day so that you can focus on positive self-affirmations, prayer time, exercise, or meditation to get your day started on a positive note.

Top Three Things (Triple "T" Approach)

Sometimes when you are faced with many tasks to complete at work or home, it can be overwhelming. You may find yourself overthinking which task to begin first. You may even get stuck just thinking about the process longer than it actually takes to complete the task(s). It's possible that you have gotten so lost in the thought process to the point of being uncertain about what you meant to do, or you may have become so overwhelmed that you talked yourself out of ever starting the task.

Perhaps, you are trying to make a decision about your career path or another life transition decision, what is keeping you stuck? Often times, the need to be perfect or sticking to what is familiar become barriers to accomplishing goals.

If your attempts to begin tasks or make decisions lead you to feeling paralyzed or emotionally incarcerated, you may be the culprit of simply getting in your way! Could you be engaging in an internal commentary that provokes fear? Fear of failure, or fear of success can sometimes stop you right in your tracks.

If you are aiming to complete certain tasks or projects, I suggest writing down the top three tasks or projects that take priority over other things that you need to complete. This makes it easier for you to focus on what's most important, so you don't become so overwhelmed. Start with the first task or project on your list. Even if you don't complete all three tasks or projects on the list right away, you will at least have started.

If you are striving to make an important decision about something that has been holding you back, try asking yourself these questions:

Am I afraid of failing? What do I believe could make me fail?

Top three things I can do as steps to face my fear to move forward in a positive and healthy direction:

1.

2.

3.

Am I afraid of succeeding? What do I believe could make me successful?

Top three things I can do as steps to embrace my success:

1.

2.

3.

As an alternative, you can also write out the top three things on the strips of paper. Fold all three of the strips of paper so that you cannot see what is written on them. Find a small box or container with a lid and place all three strips of paper inside and close the lid. When you are ready to get started, choose one of the strips of paper each day or each week and complete the task or project on that paper until all tasks or projects are accomplished. You can use this same alternative by writing the steps on the strips of paper that you plan to take to face your fear, as well as the steps to embrace your success. One of the benefits of using this strategy is that no matter where you start on your list, you will still be on a clear path to completing important tasks and goals.

Thought Stopper: "Stop in the Name of Peace."

Thought stopping is a strategy used to block and replace unwanted distressing thoughts. When you notice having distressing or intrusive thoughts, shout **"STOP!!!"** Clap your hands or snap your fingers 3 times. Replace the thoughts with a more positive thought. Your negative thought pattern is now interrupted, you did it!

The Power of Your Mind and Hands Against Anxiety

Putting the mind at ease can be done using various methods such as, breathing techniques, visual imagery, guided imagery, listening to calming music, meditation, mindfulness meditation, etc. Imagery allows you to visualize being in a place where you feel safe, calm, and happy. Many of my clients like to imagine themselves being at a beach, resting upon clouds in the sky, or at a childhood home.

Mindfulness is about being fully present and observing your thoughts and the world around you without judgment. Most of these techniques are a simple and fast way to reduce stress and provide inner peace. Another one of my favorite techniques is one that utilizes the collaboration of your mind and hands to minimize or regulate feelings of anxiety. It is a very good way to reinforce peace by reminding yourself that you are bigger than your anxiety.

To practice this exercise, get into a relaxed posture in a comfortable chair. Scan your body for any anxiety that may be present. Wherever you feel the sense of anxiety in your body, place your hand on the area of distress and take a deep cleansing breath, helping you to breathe through your anxiety. Now close your eyes and imagine that your anxiety is in the shape of a ball. Select a color that represents your ball of anxiety. On a scale of 1-10, identify how big the ball of anxiety feels to you. With your hands stretched apart in front of you, demonstrate how big the ball of anxiety feels to you. You have the power to shrink the ball of anxiety. Begin to move your hands closer together imagining that you are shrinking the ball of anxiety down to where it feels more manageable to you. You may repeat this exercise as many times as you need to bring your anxiety down as low as you can. End this exercise by breathing in relaxation and slowly exhaling, letting go of any remaining anxiety.

Use Grounding Tools to Safely Detach From Worry and Anxiety

Grounding is a practice of strategies that help you to use distraction as a way to center or anchor you to the present and to reality. When you are overwhelmed by negative emotions, grounding allows you to detach from those emotions in a safe way so that you can gain control over your emotions. We discussed in a previous chapter how coping constructively rather than destructively fosters a sense of pride and well-being.

Grounding can be done anywhere, any time, without anyone ever knowing that you are using the tools. They can be as simple as running cool or warm over your hands, holding an ice cube in your hands, pressing your heels down into the floor, saying a coping statement aloud, or thinking about names that start with the letter "s". These are just a few of the distraction tools to experience a healthy detachment from worrying.

5-4-3-2-1 Grounding

Use your five senses for a Mindfulness Countdown Moment: Slow down your thoughts and cast away your cares for 60 seconds of divine awareness. Relax in a comfortable chair or your bed. This technique is very versatile and can be utilized anywhere you go, whether you are sitting, lying down, or standing. Take a deep cleansing breath and take a look around you. Notice 5 things you can see, 4 things you can feel or touch, 3 things you can hear, 2 things you can smell and 1 thing you can taste. This exercise does a really good job at helping you stay in touch with the present. This technique also happens to be one of my favorites. Feel free to use it as often as you would like to.

"Hello Life" - Today Orientation

There are times when your mind begins to revisit the past a little too long or too often. This tends to create dreadful feelings of sadness, guilt, or loneliness. Then there are times when your mind takes a humongous leap into the future. Feelings of worry, anxiety, or fear begin to mount up within you with an intense surge of nervous energy. When either of those events occur, you may need a little help to refocus your mind to where it should be. This neat tool quickly brings you to the "here and now" by reciting the current date, time, and identifying what it is you need to be focusing on at that very moment. Essentially, you are able to bounce back into the present and greet your life today.

CHAPTER SIX

UNAPOLOGETICALLY IT'S REALLY ME, NOT YOU!

SET PERSONAL BOUNDARIES

"YOU ARE NOT REQUIRED TO SET YOURSELF ON FIRE TO KEEP OTHER PEOPLE WARM" – AUTHOR UNKNOWN

What are boundaries? When I think about boundaries, I think of a barrier or something that prevents access. I like to use this analogy when referring to boundaries - boundaries are more like fences rather than walls. While there are various definitions to describe what a boundary is, I will highlight the ones that best align with this chapter.

Boundaries can be described as a line or limit where one thing ends, and another begins; the limit of what someone considers to be acceptable behavior. Each person has different boundaries which in a sense, define who they are. Those boundaries are known as personal boundaries. The personal boundaries that we establish communicate our comfort level with something or someone.

Healthy boundaries are not established for the purpose of wall building to keep us stuck nor are they created to control or punish someone else; they are established for safety. When we are uncomfortable with something or someone, we may need to establish a boundary to protect ourselves from getting hurt by that something or someone. It is also important to be aware that there are different types of personal boundaries. Common examples of personal boundaries are physical, emotional, spiritual, financial, sexual, and time related. I will talk briefly about each of these personal boundaries.

Physical - Serve to protect your right and need for space and safety. For example, if you are standing at an ATM attempting to put in your PIN number, you would want to have some space between you and the next person standing in line for privacy and safety purposes. You may feel extremely uncomfortable if someone was standing up close to you while you were withdrawing your money. The physical distance between you and another person is a boundary. It is where you end, and they begin.

Physical boundaries can also pertain to your personal belongings such as clothing, money, vehicles, property, and your body. Imagine someone who is visiting with you deciding to go into your closet and help themselves to your toothbrush, clothing, beloved purse collection or shoes! Comfort levels vary from person to person depending upon their perceived need for physical space and safety. Consequently, when another person invades our right and need for space and safety, then our boundary has been violated or broken. Of course, when our boundary has been violated, the person who violated it is said to have crossed the line which can lead to many negative consequences. Physical boundaries may be necessary for many reasons such as privacy, safety, and health concerns.

Emotional – Invisible barriers that give you the freedom (right) to express your feelings openly and honestly without the fear of judgment, criticism or being dismissed. In a sense, it is creating a safe space to be yourself. Communicating feelings, beliefs, values, and needs can also be a way of gaining respect from others. After all, the way we treat ourselves tends to teach others how to treat us. It is here that I must give fair warning that others may not like or agree with your boundary, but that is absolutely ok because it is YOUR boundary and not theirs!

We all have different value systems and therefore think differently which is often reflected in our boundaries. With an emotional boundary being established, you can stand up for yourself and advocate for yourself freely. This is where the word "no" comes into play. While the word "no" may seem like a punishment to some people, when it is utilized to establish a boundary, it is meant for the purpose of protecting the individual who does not feel comfortable or safe. For instance, if you are at a social gathering and you need to leave early so that you can rest up for work the next day, but you are feeling pressured by a friend to hang out a little longer. In this case, you may be faced with establishing an emotional boundary by declining the request.

Another example of an emotional boundary could be refusing to allow someone else to dictate to you what you should feel, think, or do. Have you ever had a conversation with someone where you described how hurt you were feeling over a particular situation and the other person told you, "you should not feel that way;" if so, you probably felt annoyed or dismissed by their comment. Listen, you feel what you feel, and approval of what you feel is not necessary! In this situation, sharing with that person that you are uncomfortable with them telling you what you should or should not feel; and moving forward, you need for them to respect your boundary is an appropriate response.

Spiritual or Religious – Serve to protect your right and choice to worship where you choose to, as well as your belief preference and practice. Imagine someone else telling you how you should worship, where you should worship, who you should worship, and how often you should worship. This choice is reserved for you to make and be comfortable with! Projecting our values and beliefs onto others can be quite offensive. An example of a boundary in this area would be observing a religious holiday or honoring a tradition such as saying a prayer before meals even if others do not hold the same tradition.

Financial – Serve to protect your right and choice as to how you manage your finances. It is your right to set guard rails around your finances to limit how much you spend, give, loan, or borrow. It is always best practice if you are loaning or borrowing money to secure the terms of the loan in writing. When boundaries are created for financial purposes, it's usually because someone feels taken advantage of by someone else or we may want to make sure we are not setting ourselves up for a financial dilemma by taking on more debt than we may be able to handle.

Sexual – Serve to protect your right and choice to engage in personal experiences that allow you to feel respected and safe. This boundary establishes preferences such as public displays of affection, private sexual touching, contraceptive use, and sexual health history. It's also important to note that the freedom to choose involves with whom, when, where, and how often sexual contact will be made. It's extremely imperative to be sensitive in this area because what may be acceptable for one person, may not be the case for another person. For example, your partner may prefer that you wear a certain type of women's intimate apparel; however, you may find it rather offensive to do so.

Time – Reserves the right and choice as to how your time is occupied. You decide how your time will be spent, how much of your time will be spent, and with whom your time will be spent. In essence, you are the gatekeeper of your time. Establishing this boundary allows you to structure your time wisely so that you are successful in your personal goals.

Having a good understanding of what boundaries are can help you to establish healthy boundaries with others and equally respect the boundaries of other people. Others have a right to have their boundaries respected as well, even if you don't like their boundaries.

Most people have a sense of what makes them feel uncomfortable, but oftentimes the environment in which we grew up sets the tone for determining the comfort level that is experienced. If a concept is very familiar to us, we tend to be more comfortable with it when we are exposed to that concept in other areas of our lives. For instance, growing up in a large family environment where financial resources were limited could create a culture where everything had to be shared or handed down to siblings.

While you may have learned many valuable lessons to cherish, above them was "sharing." Obviously, sharing is a prized attribute to behold to the majority of people; however, the perception under which a person may have learned to share may have given them an erroneous takeaway as mentioned in Chapter Two. The takeaway lesson they may have learned is "you are a good person if you share everything." Their comfort level may be anchored higher in the area of sharing which means the compass for what is not so safe to share may not register accurately. On the other hand, a possible takeaway could also be, "I have to protect and keep everything that I have for myself because I never had anything of my own." Conversely in that case, their comfort level may be more rigid and anchored lower in the area of sharing. I am not saying that these takeaways can only be learned in an environment with limited resources or within large families.

A person who grew up in an environment where they were an only child who may have been blessed with immeasurable resources could also adopt a takeaway that they should have everything they want and do not have to share with anyone. The point is, that we all are a product of our environment in some way and things that we take away from our environment may not have been told to us by anyone, but we may have perceived it to be our truth based upon our experience and therefore, it becomes a roadmap for decision making.

When the compass for what to share or not to share is not adequately calibrated, it is also possible to lack boundaries to protect you from being harmed or to get you where you need to be. Not having boundaries has many unfortunate consequences such as being taken advantage of, being emotionally, mentally, or physically abused, losing your self identity, being frustrated, disappointed, and resentful.

Crews Nugget #6: *It is OK to not be ok with something or someone. You do not have to like or accept everything or everyone. Certain behaviors may not be tolerable or acceptable to you. You do not have to tolerate hurtful or disrespectful behavior from someone else. You have a right to establish healthy boundaries that protect you.*

Establishing healthy boundaries are essential in daily life because they protect our well-being. Healthy relationships are only as healthy as we are. As we engage in friendships, family relationships, romantic relationships, or work relationships, boundaries are necessary for assisting us in expressing our wants and needs.

Boundaries in Friendships

Friendships add value to our lives in many ways. Friends are people that we choose who know us well, we like them, and we like their company. One important aspect of friendship is the support that often comes from a proven relationship. There are other elements that we appreciate in friendships such as acceptance, encouragement, loyalty, respect, and trustworthiness.

What we value in friendships may not be the same for every woman so having a good understanding of what you value and expect out of a friendship can help you choose friends that are likely to meet your needs. Of course, you don't want to choose people who will always agree with you no matter what, but you also don't want to choose people who seem to never show you any support.

It is normal for even the closest and most long standing relationships to be tested from time to time. When situations occur that may cause you to feel hurt or disrespected in some way, knowing how to handle those uncomfortable moments can help you to salvage or to let go of the friendship. Your feelings matter but can only make a difference if you are aware of your own boundaries. Notice occasions that create discomfort or that may be hurtful to you and then explore if the situation/situations should be addressed with your friend.

If your friend's behavior "crossed the line," then your boundary was violated, and it is imperative that you communicate this to your friend, so they are aware of your boundary and that it has been broken. If your friend is not aware of your boundary, then he or she will equally not be aware that it was broken by them. Not disclosing your boundary or making it known that it was broken can lead to distance or prematurely ending friendships. It can also lead to the same behavior reoccurring because there was no knowledge of the boundary from the friend's standpoint.

Common Friendship Boundary Violations

Sharing private conversations with others

Giving habitual unconstructive criticism

Being talked about negatively behind your back

Dating a mutual love interest without having a conversation about it first

Borrowing money and not paying it back

Not being heard or listened to

Being pressured to do things that are uncomfortable for you

Expectation of friendship or loyalty when it is not given

Example Boundary

"I appreciate you being concerned about me, but I am not comfortable with you sharing personal information about me with your spouse."

"I understand things have been rough for you financially, but it's frustrating for me to continue to loan you money and you have not paid any of it back. Before I am comfortable lending you anymore money, I need for you to begin paying me back the money you already owe me."

"Unfortunately, I can't participate in the girls' Shoppe Rama trip this year because it's just not in my budget at this time."

"I feel frustrated when you share issues or concerns with me, but you seem to not often extend me the same opportunity to share any of my concerns."

"Ladies, I appreciate your invitation to attend the Karaoke Kick-Off event, but I am looking forward to my date night with _____."

Example of Boundary Enforcement

"Because you continue to share personal information about me with your husband, I am choosing to no longer share personal information with you."

Boundaries in Family Relationships

Family relationships can be one of the most difficult places in which to establish or enforce boundaries. In other relationships, we can choose whom to include in our lives, but we don't get a choice in who our family members are or will be. Family relationships can be the most amazing relationships to have.

Attending family functions and celebrating life events can provide the happiest memories we may ever experience. Our sense of loyalty can sometimes pull at our heart strings when it comes down to our interactions within family relationships. For many of us, we tend to believe that our family members will be there for us when no one else will but that is not always the case. As stated earlier, some friendships provide key components of a loving relationship that even some family members may not provide.

We can experience a feeling of guilt when considering not going along with behaviors of our family members, even when they may engage in unacceptable behavior. In some cases, our family members may have made many sacrifices for us over time or have contributed to our lives in ways that are invaluable; loyalty almost seems like the only repayment for such significant acts of kindness or generosity.

If you are a parent, the type of boundary that you establish with your kids may depend upon what is age appropriate for them. I realize you may not want to muddy the waters with your children because you want them to be your friend; however, your role is to be their parent. Remember, as you establish healthy boundaries, you are teaching them healthy boundaries. Trust me, you will have time to be their friend when they become adults, and you have more in common with them.

Some family members keep doing the same annoying or unacceptable thing that no one likes because no one wants to hurt their feelings or rub them the wrong way. But does that mean that you should ignore someone else's hurtful behavior in order to be accepted or belong? Please hear me when I say this, it's time to put an end to the generational foolery that has been going on for decades just because there are family ties. Establishing a boundary does not always guarantee that the family member will discontinue the behavior that is unacceptable to you but if they choose to continue the behavior, you can choose what your response to that behavior will be.

Family members who benefit from engaging in unacceptable behavior can also utilize manipulation or intimidation to gain support of certain behaviors that are not acceptable, which can vary in severity. Unfortunately, to this very day, there are many family secrets that have been kept but should not have been kept. Because of some family secrets that were kept, other family members may have been or will be impacted by the harmful behavior of family members that should not be tolerated or accepted.

Family members should love and want the best for its members. Wanting the best includes wanting to see its members be happy. True happiness is usually not found in conforming to who someone else wants you to be or to behave in a manner that is inauthentic. True happiness is best achieved through self-efficacy! Establishing boundaries by advocating for yourself in family relationships may not be the easiest thing to do but it can help to establish a sense of respect with others within your family. It may even help to avoid some unhealthy family patterns.

Common Family Relationship Boundary Violations

Borrowing things without asking

Going through personal belongings

Sharing personal information with another family member without permission

Intrusion on personal space or time (bathroom, bedroom, phone conversations, journals)

Inappropriate joking or put downs for pleasure

Using abusive language

Using abusive behavior

Being threatened or manipulated to do things that are not appropriate

Example Boundary

"I am not ok with you putting me down in front of my friends. I would appreciate it if you showed me more respect by speaking to me directly, in private or keep your negative comments about me to yourself"

"Just because we wear the same size in clothing, it is not ok for you to borrow my clothing without my permission. I need for you to respect my privacy and ask me if you would like to borrow any of my personal belongings."

"I know you were in a hurry on your way to school, but it is not ok for you to leave your dirty laundry on the bathroom floor. I need for you make sure that all of your personal items are put away before you leave for school."

"I always look forward to family visits, but I need for you to call me before coming over."

"You have a right to express your feelings young man/young lady, but I will not tolerate you raising your voice at me."

"Now that you are an adult, if you are going to continue to live at home, I need you to contribute to financial household responsibilities by paying the utility bill every month."

Example Boundary Enforcement

"Since you have been unable to clean up after yourself, you have communicated to me that you are not ready to take on the bigger responsibilities like having sleepovers with your friends. Unfortunately, you will have to share with your friends that you will not be able to invite them next weekend to sleep over."

Boundaries in Romantic Relationships

Establishing boundaries in romantic relationships can also be very challenging but there are many benefits to having some parameters in place. Boundaries are a two-way system: in as much as you have the right to set them, you also have to be respectful of the boundaries of others. We can't assume that any and everything goes in all romantic relationships.

Boundaries allow for safe discovery of expectations and comfort levels to avoid any misunderstandings. Starting out your relationship with clear boundaries can ensure that you are reading from the same page in a book.

There are various romantic relationship types to consider when establishing boundaries. All boundaries may not be appropriate for every romantic relationship type. It is very important to understand what your needs are and what is acceptable to you. Some common types of romantic relationships include, but not limited to dating relationships, situationships, open relationships, committed relationships, and marriage.

In today's world, dating relationships can have different meanings. Generally, dating can be described as two people in an intimate relationship. The relationship does not have to be a sexual one.

In situationship dating, the two people involved are known to be "just kickin it" or "hanging out", for now! There is usually more of an emotional connection and sexual involvement; however, it is without a commitment to each other. A situationship is also known to be quite complicated in that it is not defined by the parties and lacks consistency. This type of relationship is said to differ from a "friends with benefits" arrangement.

The word "friends" in a friends with benefits scenario sets the tone that you simply will not cross over the friendship zone! Although the sexual benefits may be exciting and there could even be an emotional connection, there is usually a mutual understanding that commitment is not included on the to-do-list.

Ladies, I almost want to do a poll at this point to see whom is still following me so far and whom I have lost! (chuckling). Well, there is not much guess work in the description of an open relationship. I'm certain that the word "open" clearly gives it away! It simply means having more than one romantic or sexual partner at a time. An agreement of non-exclusivity is made by the parties included.

Committed relationships are based on an agreement between two partners being committed to one another. They are typically long-term relationships and involve love, trust, honesty, respect, as well as other positive qualities. The exclusivity that both partners commit to in their relationship tends to create a sense of closeness and security.

Because a marital relationship is also a committed relationship, it offers the same positive qualities listed above. In addition, marital relationships are based on a legal or formally recognized union of two people also known as matrimony or wedlock. The bond established is pledged for a lifetime which provides a futuristic outlook for mutual goals, family planning, stability and growing old together as a couple.

Relationships of any kind can be hard work at times. It can certainly be scary to draw the line in the sand especially when your heart is tied to the line. You may be afraid that your needs may not be respected or even dismissed. Having tough conversations does not come easy for most people. You may struggle with the gut-wrenching fear that your partner will end the relationship if you establish a boundary. Insecurity and fear of abandonment can sometimes keep you stuck in lifeless, self-sacrificing, unfulfilling, or abusive relationships.

Sometimes what stands in the way of establishing boundaries in relationships is low self-esteem or low self-worth. There is a direct correlation between self-worth and boundaries. The higher your self-esteem is or the more that you value yourself and your rights, the more likely you are to establish boundaries that communicate your needs and expectations to others. By the same token, boundary setting can improve your self-esteem. Standing up for yourself and making choices that are best for your well-being is such a confidence booster! Remember, boundaries define you and they protect you.

It is also wise to keep in mind that without establishing healthy boundaries, your relationship may be at risk for becoming aimless and lacking substance. For relationships that are intended to lack definition or labels, that is okay too, as long as both people are aware of those limits. Regardless of which type of romantic relationship you may have, communication is key in all relationships.

I think it's worth saying at this point that being in a romantic relationship does not mean that you must give up all rights to maintaining your own identity. Even in marriage, there is a sensitive balance of growing individually yet developing a deep rooted and emotional bond with your partner. As a matter of fact, it is necessary to maintain your individuality for the success of a romantic relationship. In a nutshell, that simply means you should continue doing things that you enjoy or make you happy. For instance, if you enjoyed pampering yourself with manicures prior to being in a relationship, then continuing to make that a part of your life while involved in a romantic relationship will help you stay plugged into you so that you are not vulnerable to losing yourself in your partner.

The same would be true if you enjoyed girls' night social outings or women's group activities prior to being in a romantic relationship, it is emotionally healthy for you to continue to nurture those friendships while being involved in a romantic relationship. It is also a good idea to set aside some "me time" for yourself individually. All relationships need personal space sometimes, yes, even romantic ones. Spending too much time together without any personal time can create a sense of feeling smothered and the desperate need for space. In other words, establish an understanding with your partner that allows for independence and autonomy.

Continue to pursue your dreams and goals so that you will be happy with yourself. If you are not happy with yourself, chances are that you will not be happy in a relationship either. If by chance, you are in a romantic relationship where your partner does not respect your autonomy, then it may be time to establish a boundary by letting your partner know what works for you and what does not.

If you are feeling like you are on the brink of compromising your values, hobbies, dreams, goals, or self-respect, consider asking yourself this question: Do I have to lose who I am so that my partner will accept or love me? If you give up your identity, then who will your partner be in a relationship with....not you! Unfortunately, in some cases, relationships may eventually come to an end if needs and boundaries are not being respected.

Lastly, ladies, please do not buy into the insecurity of a partner who tells you, "no one else will ever want or love you." This is a news flash for you so DO NOT turn the channel, listen up......they wanted you before you got into a relationship with them and somebody else will want you, love you, and even respect you when they are out of the picture.

Common Romantic Relationship Boundary Violations

Having a romantic or emotional relationship with someone else outside of the relationship with your partner

Stalking or harassment

Being deceptive or gaslighting

Invading your partner's private information or space

Sharing private or personal information without your permission

Touching your partner's body physically or sexually without permission

Physical abuse

Insults or verbal aggression

Example Boundary

"I understand that you are frustrated by our conversation, however, I will not tolerate you interrupting or yelling at me."

"I am really uncomfortable with meeting you at your house for our first date, I prefer to meet up at a restaurant for lunch or dinner."

"I am not ok with you offering your ex-girlfriend/ex-wife to stay at your apartment during her visit for a work conference. I need for you to be respectful of my feelings and allow her to make alternative lodging arrangements.

"I am not comfortable being intimate while guests are in our home."

" I attend a book club social on Wednesday evenings, so please do not make any plans for us on those nights."

Example Boundary Enforcement

"If you continue to interrupt or yell at me, I will discontinue the conversation and walk away."

Boundaries in the Workplace

Whether you work from home virtually or in an actual office building, you may have found it easy to do without even noticing that you are spending on average 8.5 - 9 hours a day working. You may have even put in some work time on the weekends. If that is the case, more of your 24-hour day may be spent working than the 8 hours of sleep that is recommended for your well-being.

Work is important and should be valued for a number of reasons. Work, for many of us, allows us to have a sense of security to provide for our families. We can develop a sense of meaning and purpose by applying ourselves and learning new things to successfully perform our jobs. Financial security from working also allows us to contribute to something larger than ourselves.

Other perks from work afford us the opportunity to make new friends and to engage in leisurely activities outside of work. While work plays a vital role in our journey of life, having a healthy work-life balance allows enrichment along the way. A good and simple definition for work-life balance is the amount of time you spend doing your job versus the amount of time you spend doing what's important to you outside of work.

The benefits to having this healthy balance is far too great to ignore. A few of these surprising benefits are increased productivity, better time management, reduction in sickness and absenteeism, a less stressful work environment, increased motivation and commitment, improved physical and mental health, and overall well being. To gain the balance and the benefits will require establishing healthy boundaries.

You may need to familiarize yourself with the concepts of "no" or "not now" as a way to accomplish this goal. This also means that you may have to make some necessary changes to your work ethics and your personal time allotment. For starters, if you are a "yes" woman to everything and everyone, but very seldom say "yes" to you, then you are not establishing healthy limits to protect your well-being. There is nothing wrong with staying late at work to complete a task or assignment that has a hard upcoming deadline; however, if this becomes your norm, you may be placing yourself in a position to come up immensely short in your personal life.

When your work habits consistently keep you from attending doctor's appointments, socializing with family and friends, taking care of parenting responsibilities, or accomplishing personal goals, you are less likely to be happy with your job. It's important to assess your workload and the time that may be required to complete your tasks. It may be necessary for you to brainstorm with your boss or staff to prioritize tasks or delegate some of your tasks to other co-workers.

You may be doing a great job at work, but how long will that last before you are overwhelmed and at your wits end. Burnout can occur as a result of emotional, mental, and physical exhaustion brought on by prolonged or repeated stress. Even though burnout can be experienced in other areas of life such as parenting and caretaking, it is often caused by problems at work. In the event that parenting or caretaking responsibilities prevent you from being as flexible with your schedule as you would like to be, it is important to discuss time constraints with your boss or other staff so that they are aware of your availability.

It's good to know what helps you to be more productive when working so you can be successful. Pay attention to how you feel during the day emotionally and physically to make sure that you are not overextending yourself. Establish set hours that you work. Being intentional about blocking scheduled time for lunch breaks can help to replenish your mind and energy. It also teaches others to be respectful of your time. You may have to delay a meeting or request that a meeting be delayed so that you can take care of your physical and emotional well-being.

It can also be challenging at times to work toward goals in the workplace that include many different people with many different personalities. Goals can sometimes depend on others to some extent directly or indirectly. Quite frankly, personalities don't always match and neither do the qualifications. Navigating around how to respect the opinions of others can be difficult. Personal property, personal and physical space of others also must be equally respected.

The work environment should be a "safe" space in which you enter for the purposes of performing your professional duties. You may not like your co-worker, colleague, or boss, but if you want to keep your job, you do have to maintain a professional and respectful relationship with them. This can be easier said than done, right? Things can be said or done that can rub you the wrong way and attitudes can flare up if you are not careful. You can certainly address something that is said or done to you that makes you feel uncomfortable; however, how you decide to express your concern or how the concern of someone else is expressed to you is where things can get dicey.

As you may know, it is not always what is said but how it is said that tends to create most conflict. If you are the communicator of information or a concern, try to place yourself in that person's shoes first. Secondly, take a deep breath and then communicate in a manner that you would appreciate being spoken to.

To be honest with you, I strongly suggest using the "HALT" Method prior to interacting with others. This awesome tool was developed by David Streem, MD, as a way to help people recognize their personal triggers which may lead to unhealthy behaviors.

H – Hungry

A – Angry

L – Lonely

T – Tired

I find that I am a much better listener when I engage in some quality self-care time to perform this little tune-up when needed. Do yourself a favor by partaking in a quick check in with yourself to assess what your needs are and then actually address them! If you are struggling in any of these areas that I mention above, your communication may be far from attentive or effective. It may be necessary to eat a nutritional snack, go for a brief walk, call a friend for emotional support, or take a moment to relax by listening to soft music. These are all healthy ways to address your needs and nourish your well-being.

It may also be a good idea to write out what you would like to say prior to having the conversation. This gives you an opportunity to have a quick preview of what you want to communicate. Taking a look at what you have written down on paper allows you to establish some "safe emotional distance" between you and the other person while you are trying to gather your thoughts, without the risk of being judged or attacked verbally. You may even choose to revise what you have written so that you do not come across in an aggressive, rude, sarcastic, or insensitive manner.

As stress intensifies from the pressures of life from work, relationships, parenting, finances, and a myriad of other challenges, choosing healthy out-lets are essential to balancing work and personal life. It is beneficial to take planned time off from work to relax or go on a vacation. According to com munity.thriveglobal.com, a 2,000 participant study conducted by OnePoll, found that 62 percent of American Workers were worried their bosses would judge them for taking mental health days off. Under this same source, a recent survey revealed that only 51 percent of Americans take their paid vacation time. Trust me, it does not mean that you are not a good employee or boss if you are not accommodating everyone all the time! You will be a much better employee or boss when you feel like you have had an opportunity to get your emotional needs met by taking some time away from work to recharge.

There may be times when meeting certain demands are crucial but there will be times when you are unable to or unwilling to meet the demand when it places you at risk emotionally or physically. Working smarter so that your workload is not overwhelming is a key component here. Asking for what you want rather than demanding it or intimidating others often goes a long way. You know there is a saying that, "you can get more flies with honey than with vinegar."

If you are the person being communicated to, still take a deep breath, and truly listen to understand what is being said prior to responding, without interrupting them. If you feel uncomfortable about what was said or how it was presented to you, you have a right to share that concern, but it should be shared respectfully and directly to the person that you have the concern with.

Common Workplace Boundary Violations

Touching someone without permission

Use of intimidation or constant monitoring that interferes with work responsibilities

Becoming friends on Facebook with Supervisors, Managers, or Bosses

Romantic relationship with a co-worker

Disclosing personal or confidential information without permission

Violating others' boundaries

Being asked or asking for work to be completed during non-working hours

Use of insensitive or offensive language

Example Boundary

"Unfortunately, I am only able to contribute $20 to the sunshine fund this year.

"If you have any questions or concerns regarding this project, please make me aware before the end of the day, because I do not respond to text or emails on the weekend."

"I understand that you are experiencing some personal family challenges, but it is unacceptable for you to lash out at your co-workers and use offensive language toward them."

"While I appreciate the opportunity given to me to take the lead role on this project; however, it feels very dismissive toward me to not be invited to meetings where my projects are being discussed. I would like to be included in any meetings that involve my projects."

"I am happy to facilitate the presentation on Work-Personal Life Balance, but I will need enough notice so that I will have adequate time to prepare."

"Unfortunately, I am unable to work after 5:00 pm because I need to be on time to pick up my kids before the daycare closes."

"My colleagues have been given an opportunity to participate in the Leadership Program to help prepare them for senior management roles within the company, I would appreciate the opportunity to participate in the Leadership Program so that I can prepare for advancement as well."

Example Boundary Enforcement

"As discussed in our previous conversation, my workload is very overwhelming. I really need some time to get caught up or gain assistance with my workload. If I am not provided with additional assistance or time to get caught up, I will be unable to meet the project deadline."

Crews Nugget #7: If you feel that your boundary has been crossed, don't assume it was intentional! Use it as a teaching moment to express to the other person how they came across to you, or how their behavior impacted you, and what you need from them as a result.

My Personal Unapologetic Boundaries

Someone I want to establish a boundary with:

I will establish my boundary by telling them:

Someone I want to enforce my boundary with:

I will enforce my boundary by telling them:

Boundary Pearls of Wisdom

- Everyone has a right to establish boundaries.

- It is not necessary to defend yourself or over-explain.

- Don't accept someone's invitation to a shouting match. Excuse yourself if the conversation becomes too heated.

- Be prepared to follow through on boundaries that you have established.

- If you are setting boundaries, communicate what is (un)comfortable or (un)acceptable to you.

- Be **c**lear, be **c**onfident, be **c**onsistent, and be **f**irm – (CCCF).

- It is always a good idea to ask rather than assume what is comfortable or acceptable to others.

- Do not mix work with personal time.

- If you have invaded someone else's boundary, immediately acknowledge it, and apologize; then correct the issue.

- If someone has established a boundary with you, respect it even if you don't like it.

- Be respectful of space, physical touch, personal property, and the opinions of others.

- No means, No! There are many ways to say "No" without ever using the word.

I hope that you have enjoyed reading this book and that you were able to take away something useful to manage your stress. I also hope that reading this book gives you a more courageous and assertive voice if you feel that you have never had one. It may be necessary to seek out professional counseling or a psychiatrist for medication in some cases if your stress or anxiety is unmanageable. Giving yourself the proper care that you need is a sign of strength and self-love.

As a reminder, by making yourself a priority, you can expect to be the best version of yourself possible. Placing yourself as a priority is the first step you can take to ensure that your happiness and overall well-being is achieved. Making yourself a priority does not mean that you don't care about other people, but rather, that you are mindful that you can't be there for others until you are able to be there for yourself.

When life becomes hectic, most women forget to just slow down and breathe. There will always be something on your to do list, but relaxation should be one of them. Relaxation lessens the stress effects on your mind and body. Relaxation allows you to unwind and connect with a moment of peace and solitude. Relaxing also allows you to gain clarity during some of life's most challenging times so that you can reset your mind.

Incorporating exercise or "movement" regularly into your daily or weekly routine offers immediate and long-term health benefits. As you already know, one size does not fit all so design your workout to fit you. Exercise in any form can act as a stress reliever! Ladies, it is ok to aim high as high-definition women often do, but do not aim so high that you set yourself up for unnecessary feelings of disappointment and failure.

Being in control of your life and establishing realistic expectations for yourself will help to keep your stress level in check. Simply allow other people's expectations for you to remain *their* expectations! Their expectations of you don't have to be yours unless you want them to be. You are unique, vibrant, beautiful, and intelligent with a whole life filled with meaningful experiences that define you, so no one else ever needs to take on the responsibility of doing that for you!

It can be easy to burn out quickly from anything when you are taking on way more than you should. Some areas of your life may require a reset so that you are in control of what's on your plate. Creating healthy boundaries is a rewarding way to practice self-care, gain self-respect and to navigate your way around relationships personally and professionally.

Lastly, I recommend that you read this book over and over and keep it as a handy reference tool so that you are always on top of your stress level. Keep in mind that the strategies I discussed throughout this book may not suit every woman, however I can guarantee that they definitely will not work if you do not use them. Now that you have tools to help you to feel more comfortable in your own shoes, it's time for you to *kick the **"s"** out of your stress!*

How TO Kick The "S" Out of Stress
Notes

_____

_____

_____

_____

_____

_____

_____

_____

_____

_____

_____

_____

_____

_____

_____

_____

_____

How TO Kick The "S" Out of Stress
Notes

_____

_____

_____

_____

_____

_____

_____

_____

_____

_____

_____

_____

_____

_____

_____

_____

_____

_____

How TO Kick The "S" Out of Stress
Notes

How TO Kick The "S" Out of Stress
Notes

_____

_____

_____

_____

_____

_____

_____

_____

_____

_____

_____

_____

_____

_____

_____

_____

_____

_____

_____

How TO Kick The "S" Out of Stress
Notes

How TO Kick The "S" Out of Stress
Notes

_____

_____

_____

_____

_____

_____

_____

_____

_____

_____

_____

_____

_____

_____

_____

_____

FURTHER READING

1. Chapman, Gary. (2010). The 5 Love Languages: The Secret to Love that Lasts. Northfield Publishing.

2. Cloud, Henry, Dr. & Townsend, John, Dr. (2017). Boundaries Updated and Expanded Edition: When to Say Yes, How to Say No to Take Control of Your Life. Zondervan Publication.

3. Mayo Clinic Staff. (2024). Relaxation Techniques: Try These To Lower Stress. Healthy Lifestyle Stress Management. http://www.mayoclinic.org/healthy-lifestyle/stress-manage ment/in-depth/relaxation-technique/art-20045368.

4. Mayo Clinic Staff. (2021). Exercise: 7 Benefits of Regular Physical Activity. Healthy Lifestyle Fitness. http://www.mayoclinic.org/healthy-lifestyle/fitness/in-dept h/exercise/art-20048389.

5. Najavits, L. (2002). Seeking Safety: A Treatment Manual for PTSD and Substance abuse. Guilford Publications.

6. Robinson, Bryan, Ph.D. (2021). American Workers Are Afraid To Take Time Off. Thrive Global. http://www.community.thrive.global.com.

7. Weil, Andrew, MD. 4-7-8 Breathing Exercises.
   http://www.drweil.com/videos-features/breathing-exercis
   es-4-7-8.

8. Wright, Ben. (2019). 8 Reasons Why Everyone Should Embrace a Mini-Vacation. Thrive Global.
   http://www.community.thrive.global.com.

ABOUT THE AUTHOR

Samantha Tubbs-Crews is a Licensed Mental Health Counselor/Psychotherapist who has worked in the mental health field for over 29 years. She has been in private practice for the past 24 years. She received a Master's Degree in Mental Health Counseling from Nova Southeastern University in 1997. She holds various certifications with designation as a National Certified Counselor, Qualified Clinical Supervisor, Certified Employee Assistance Professional, and Certified Clinical Trauma Professional.

She enthusiastically serves a diverse population and works with a number of life issues such as depression, bipolar, anxiety, grief, stress, marriage, and couples counseling. Her specialty is in trauma recovery. She also enjoys facilitating seminars/workshops focusing on Women Empowerment, Marital Enrichment, Work-Personal Life Balance, Self-Care, Communication Skills, Boundary Setting, Conflict Resolution, and a host of others. She is very passionate about mental health advocacy and empowering others.

She has made appearances as a keynote speaker at corporate events, educational institutions, religious conferences, retreats, and teen forums. In her leisure time, Samantha enjoys cruising, music, art, craft projects, mindfully walking, and spending quality time with family members and friends. She is married to the man of her dreams, and together they have four wonderful children and one awesome grandchild.

Samantha's inspiration for writing this book came from many clients who often told her that they wished they could carry her around so that when certain situations came up, they would have her voice of wisdom to deal with their challenge at hand.

TO connecT wITH samanTHa

Email: Empoweredmindzbooks@gmail.com
Website: www.Empoweredmindz.com
Facebook: Empoweredmindz

www.ingramcontent.com/pod-product-compliance
Lightning Source LLC
Chambersburg PA
CBHW062112080426
42734CB00012B/2840